Flights of Fancy:
Magical Creatures to Color

By Robin Joy Andreae

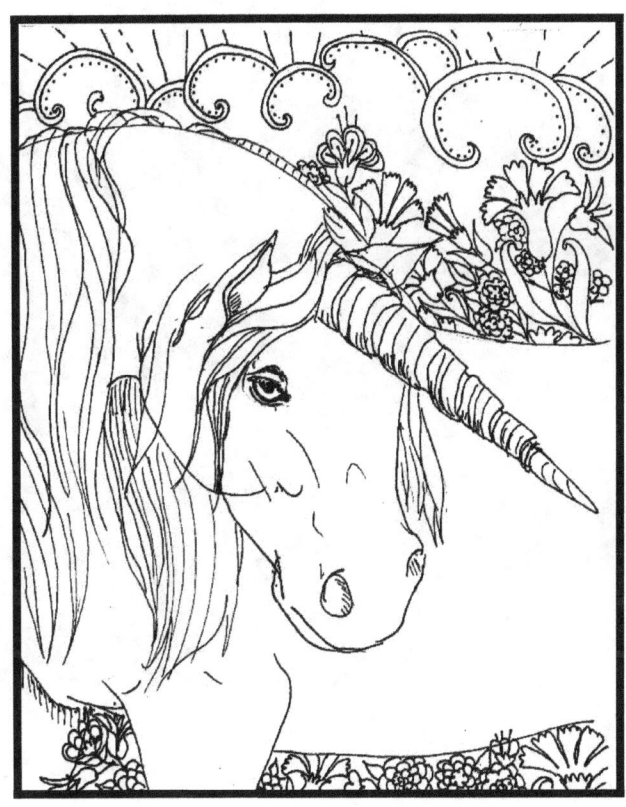

Copyright 2016 Robin Joy Andreae
ISBN-13: **978-1530315758**
ISBN-10: **1530315751**

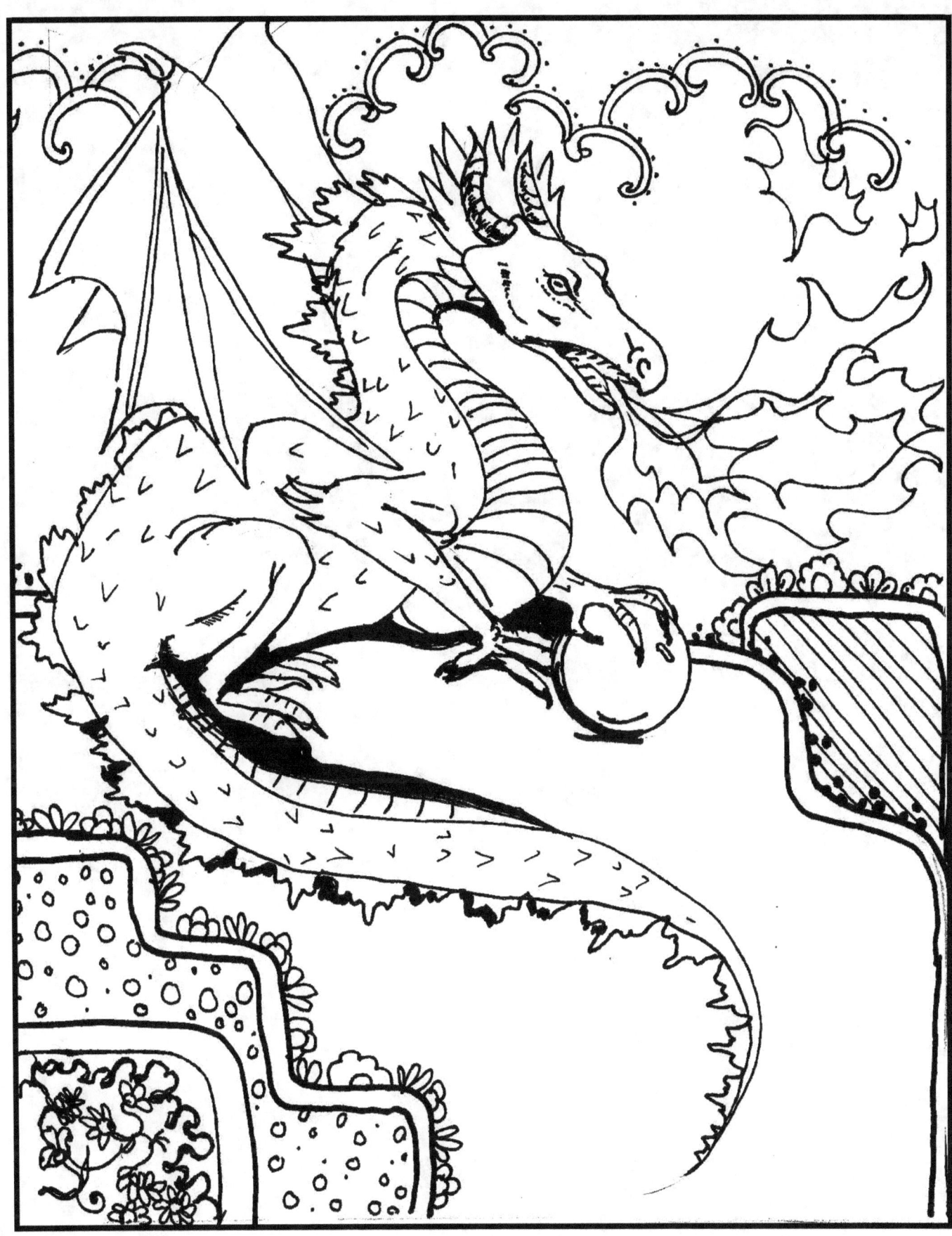

Figure 1 Fire in the Sky

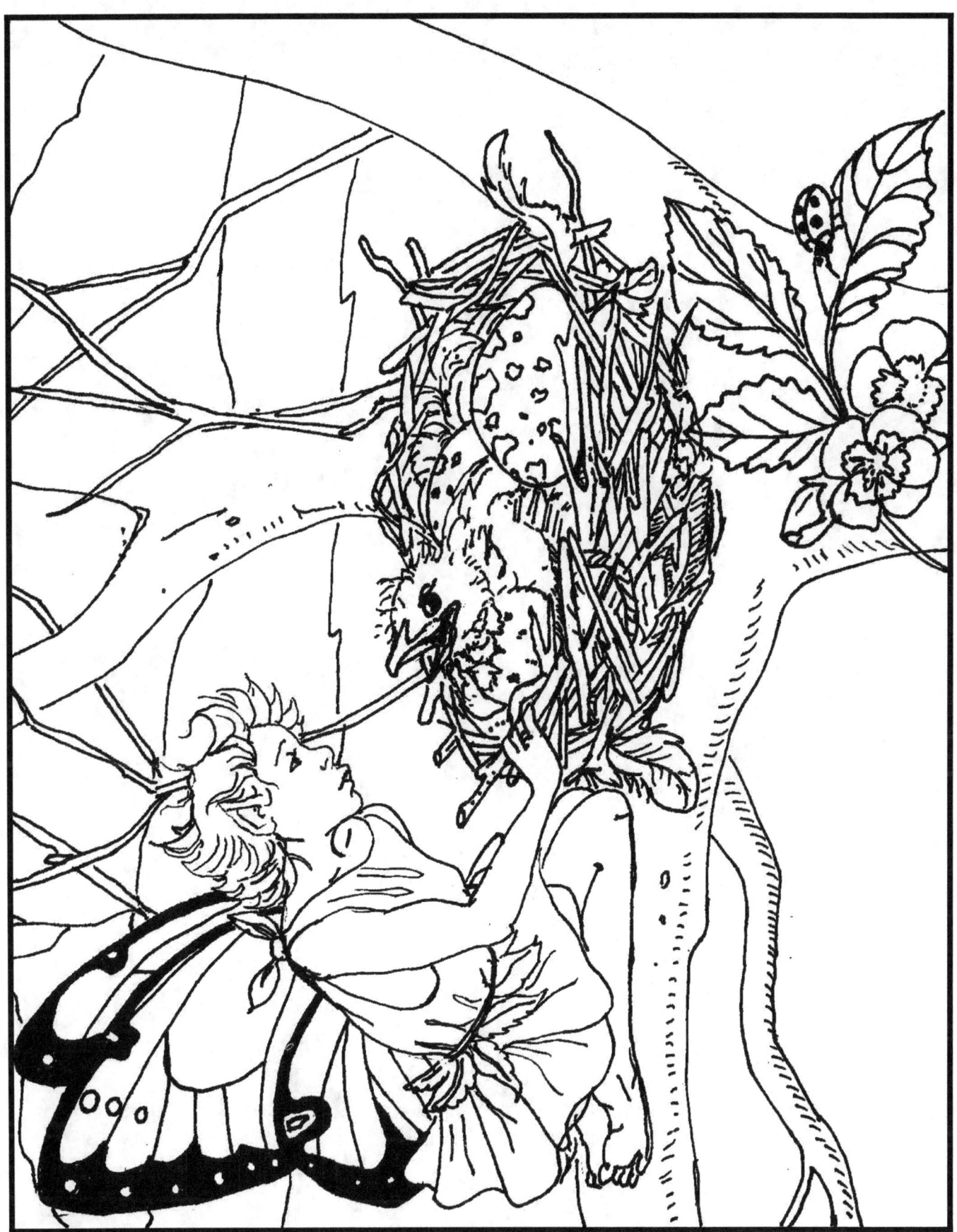

Figure 2 Spring

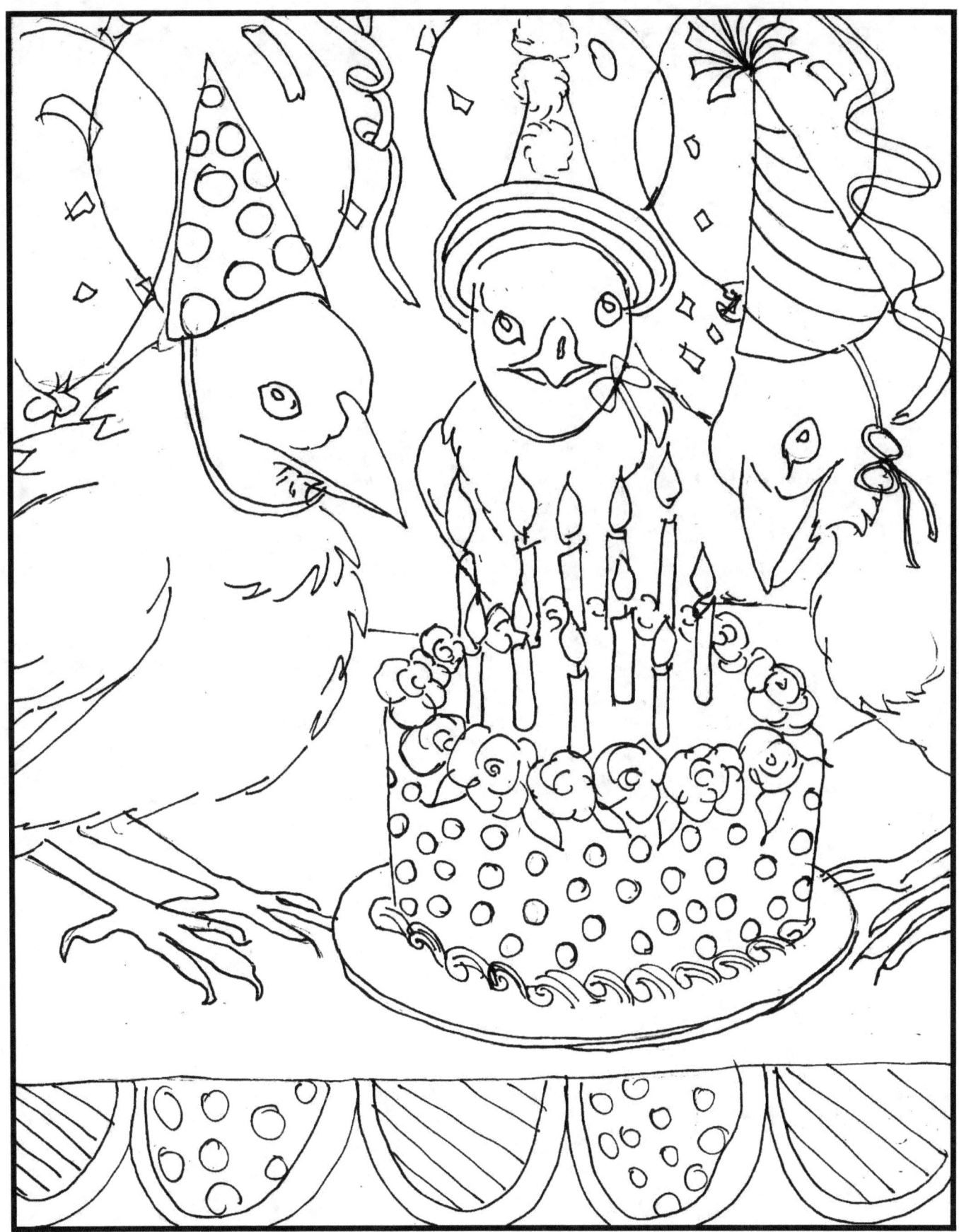

Figure 3 Bird-Day Party

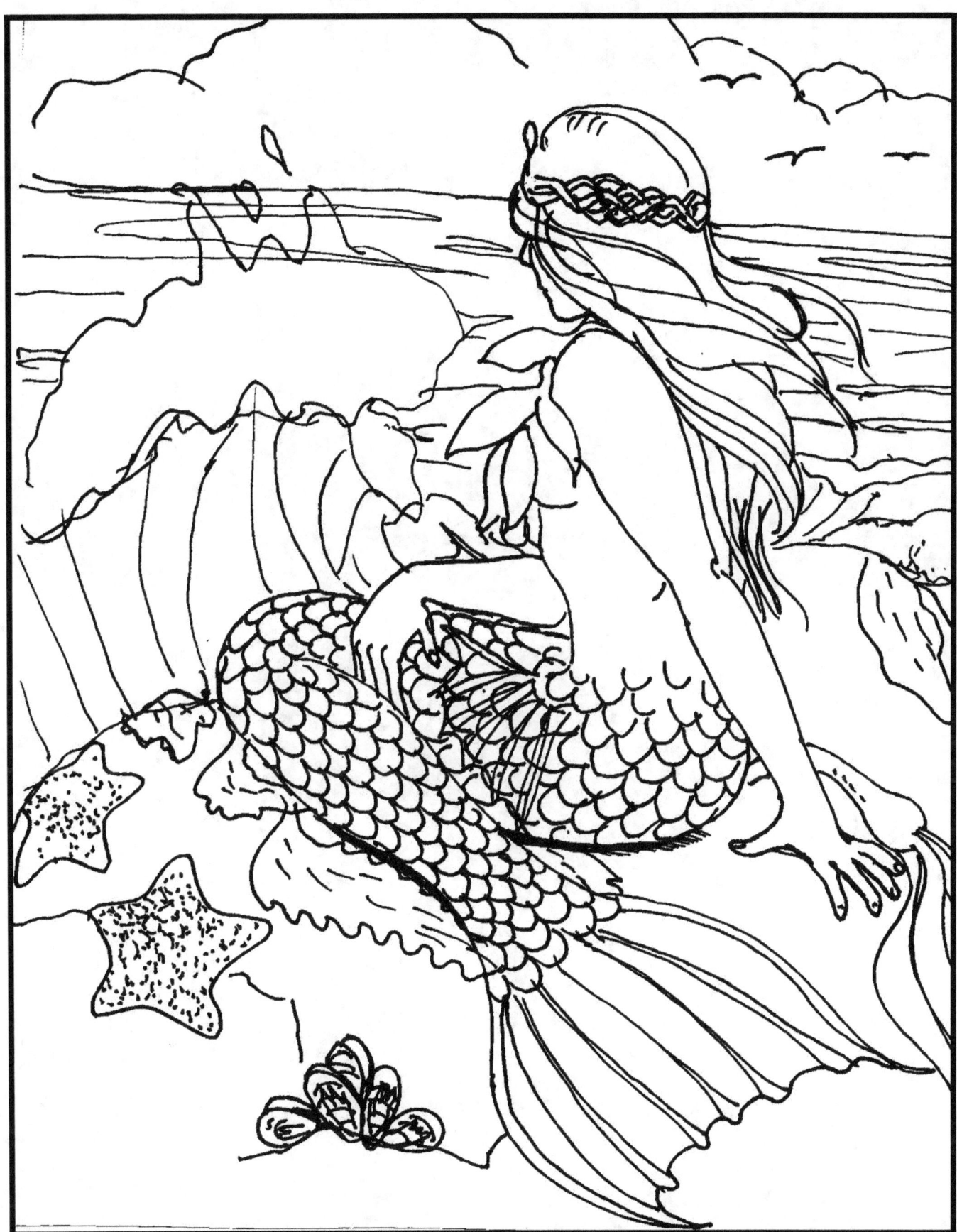

Figure 4 Resting on the Rock

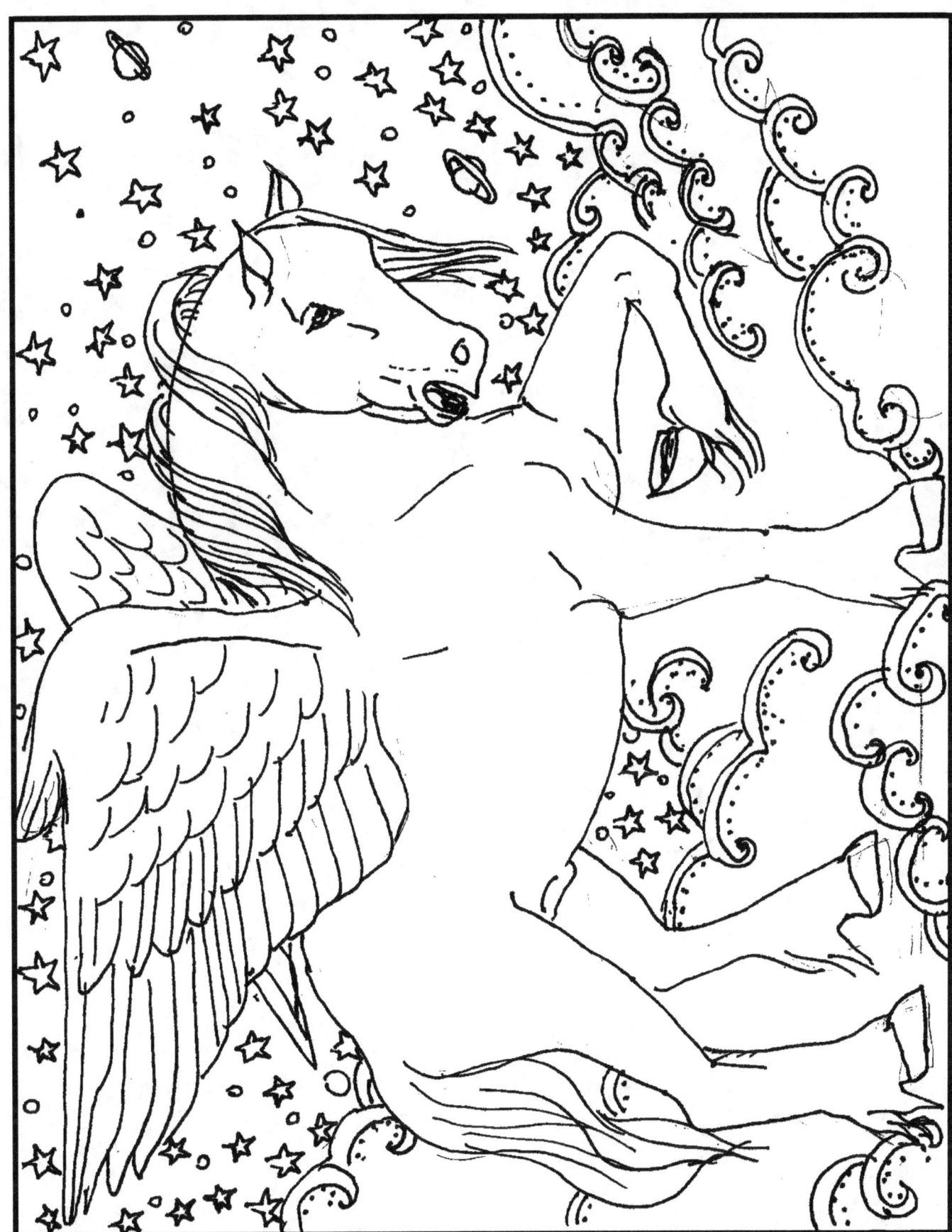

Figure 5 Winged Majesty

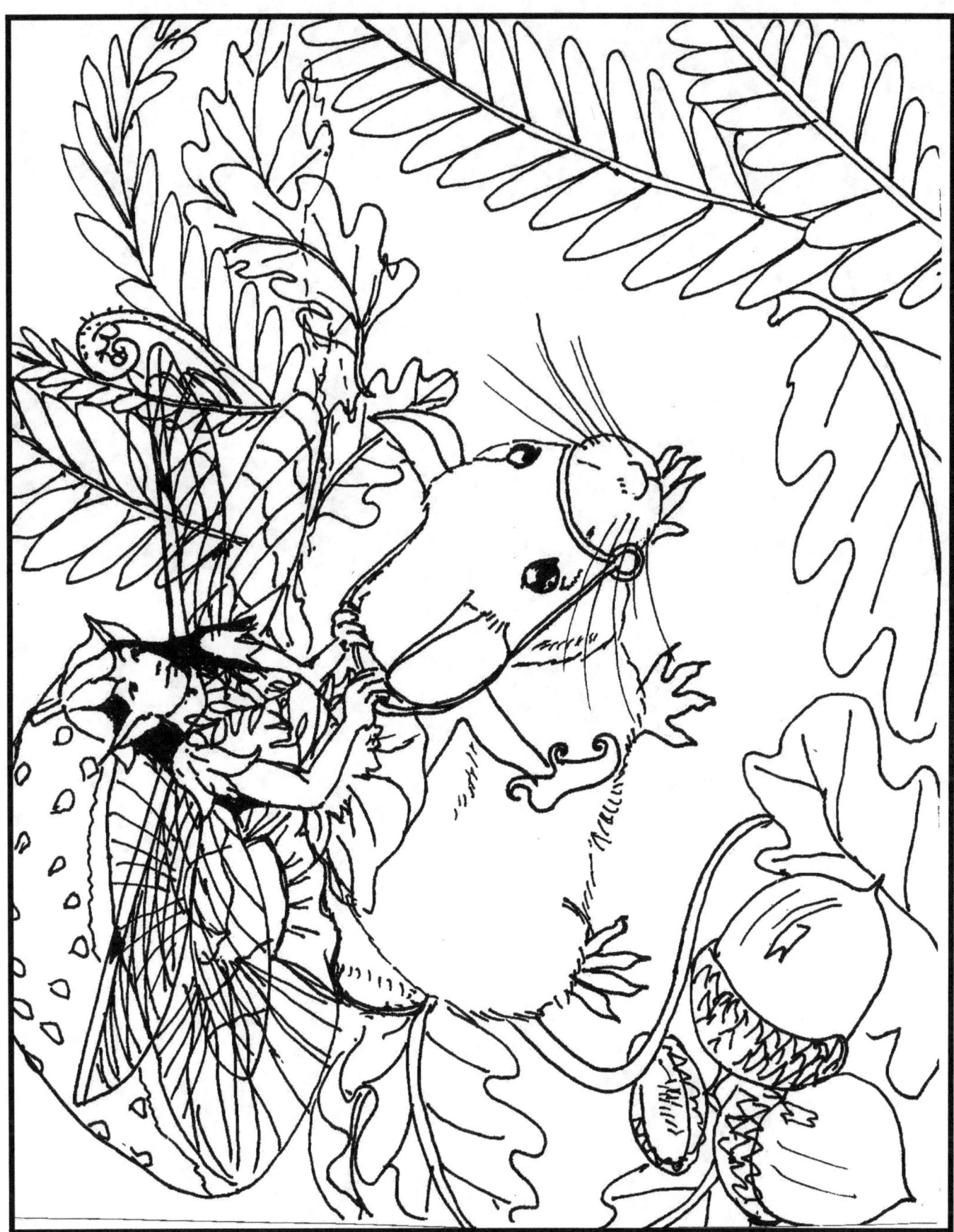

Figure 6 Morning Ride

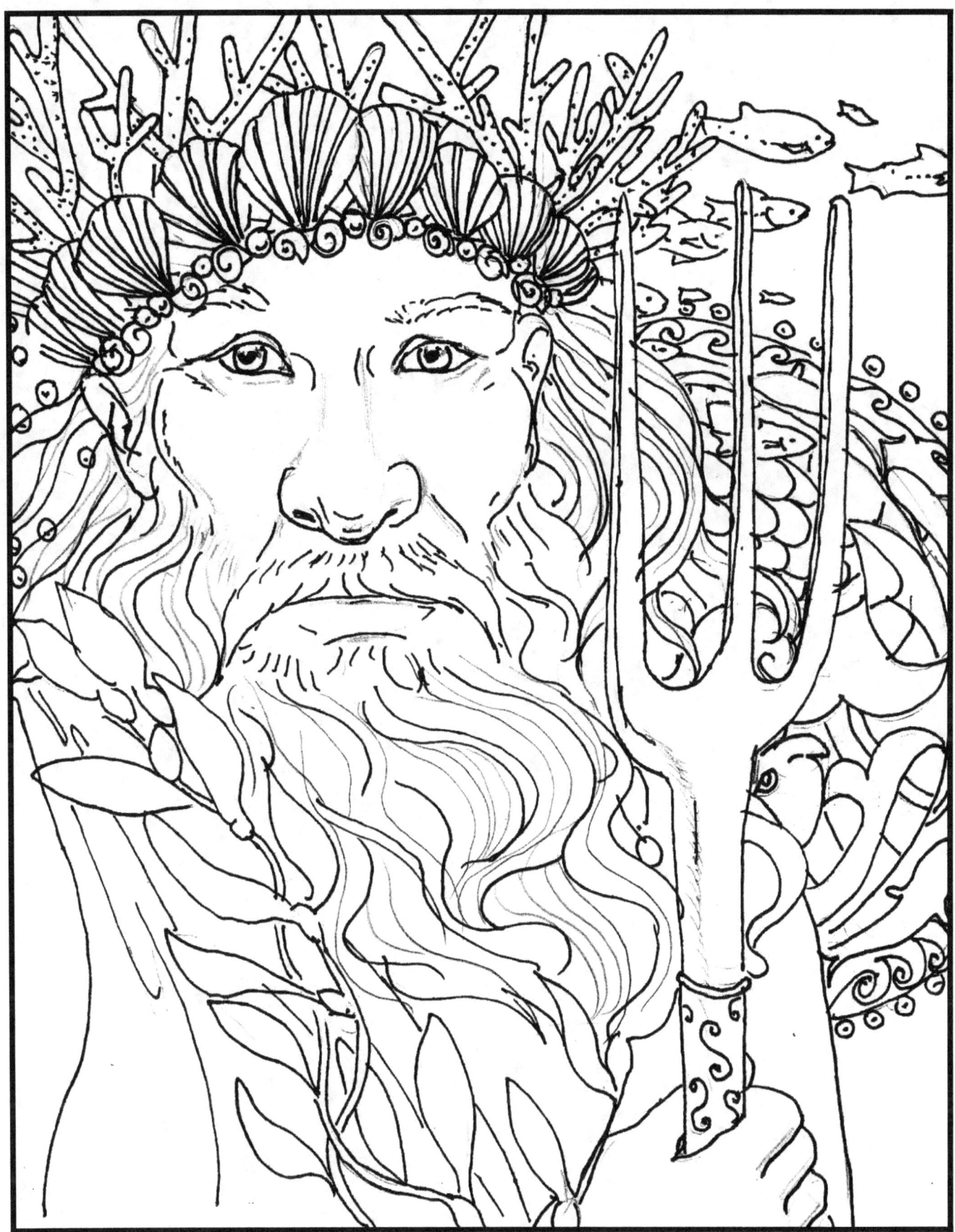

Figure 7 Poseidon

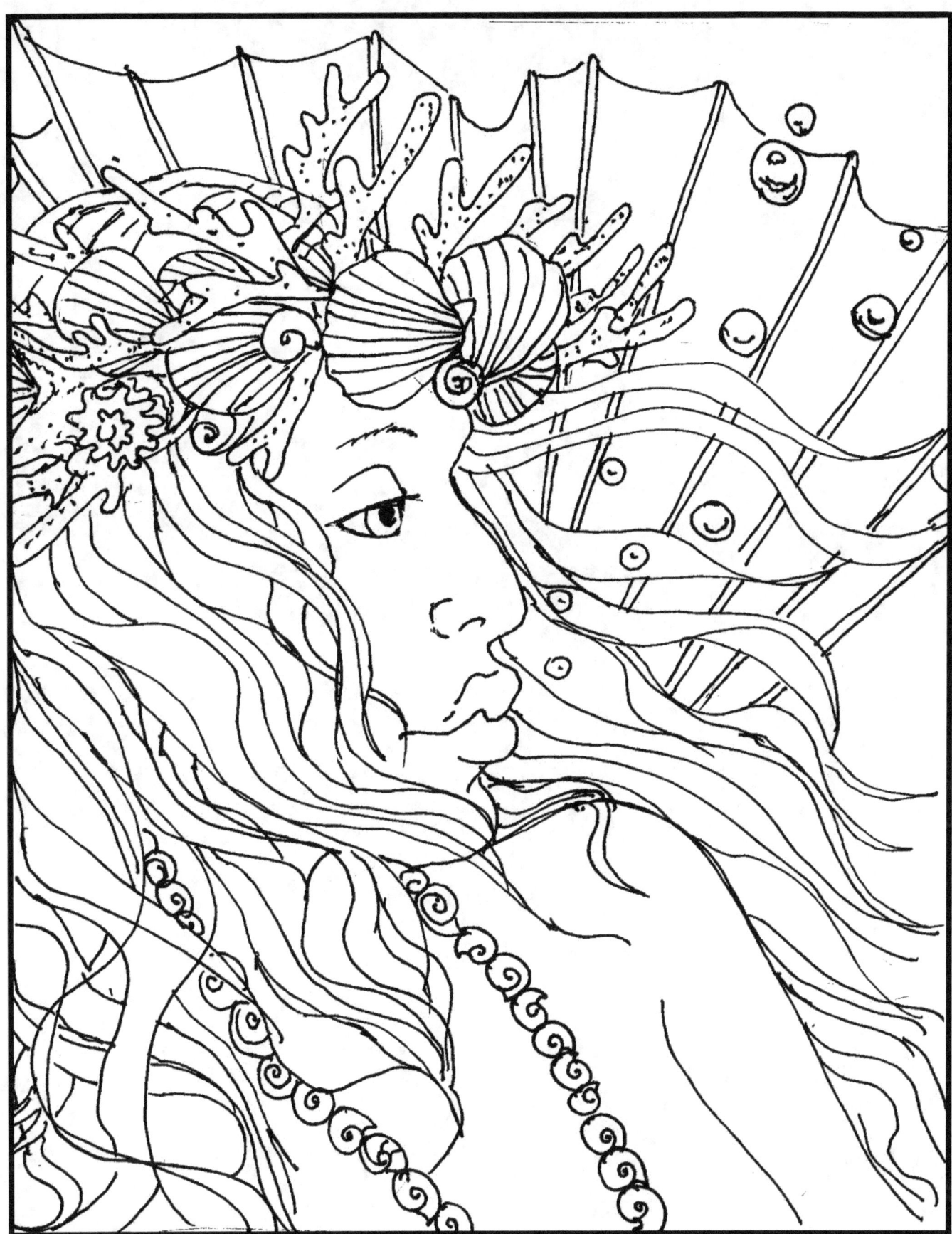

Figure 8 Mermaid

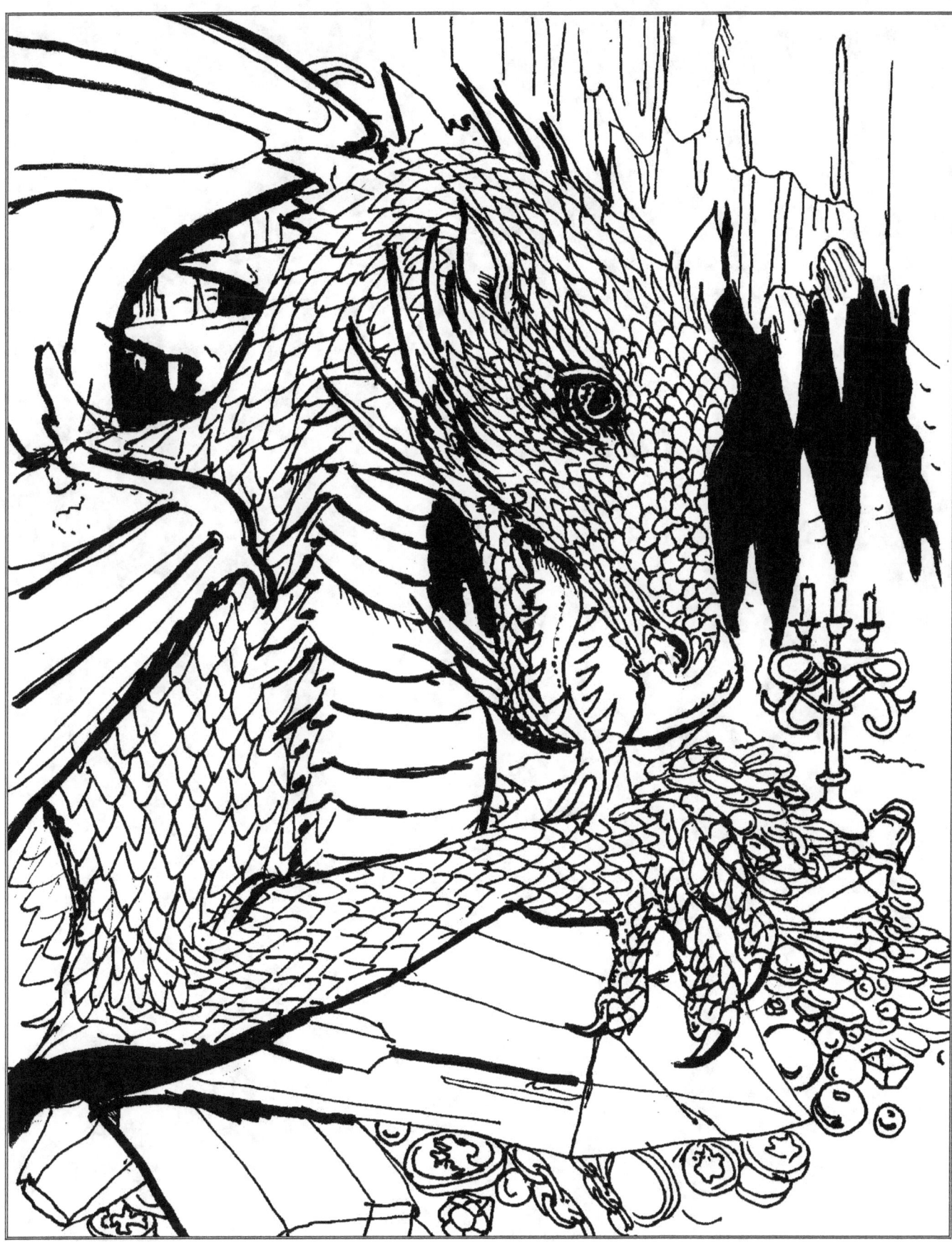

Figure 9 Mine

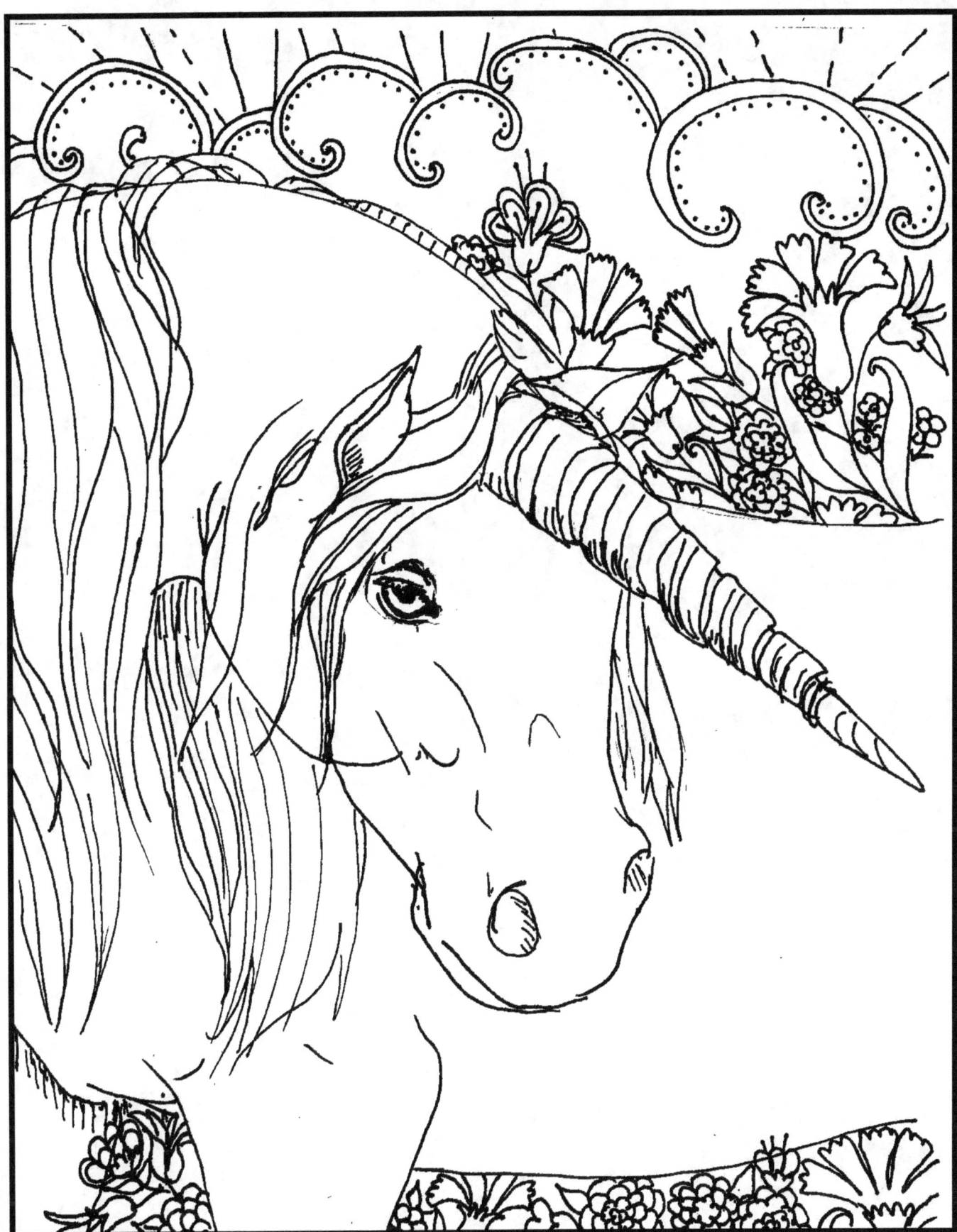

Figure 10 Magic Morning

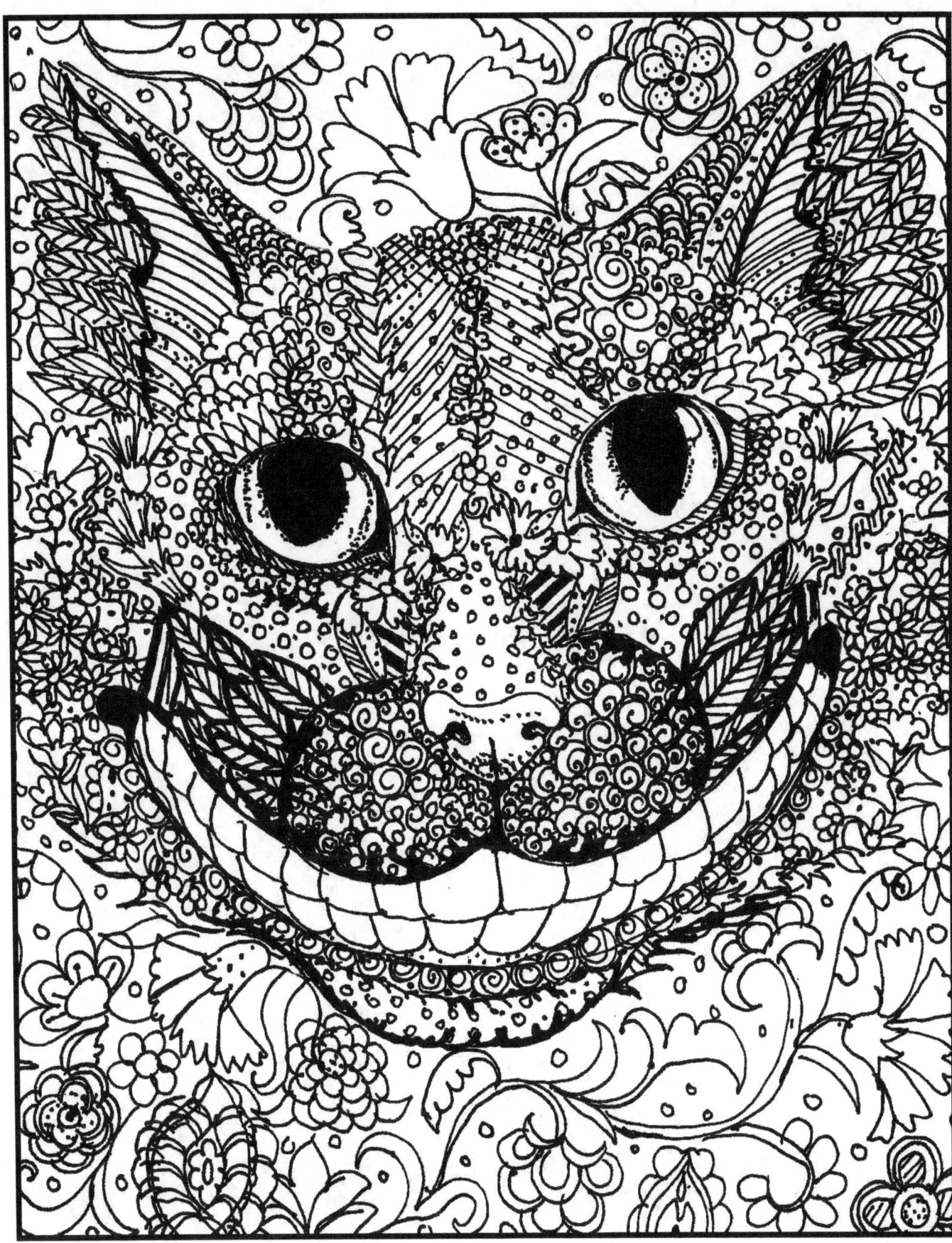

Figure 11 A Winning Smile

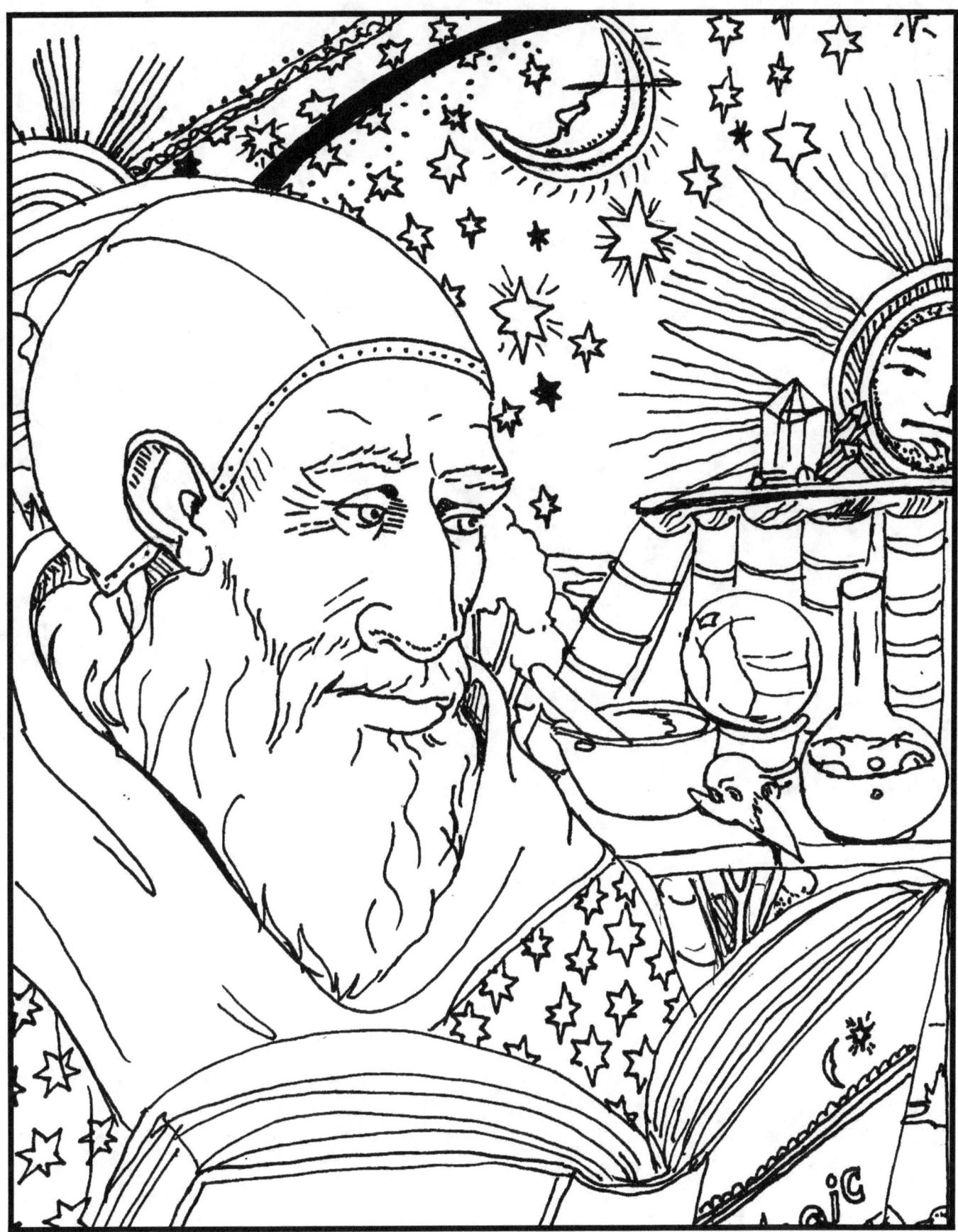

Figure 12 The Wizard

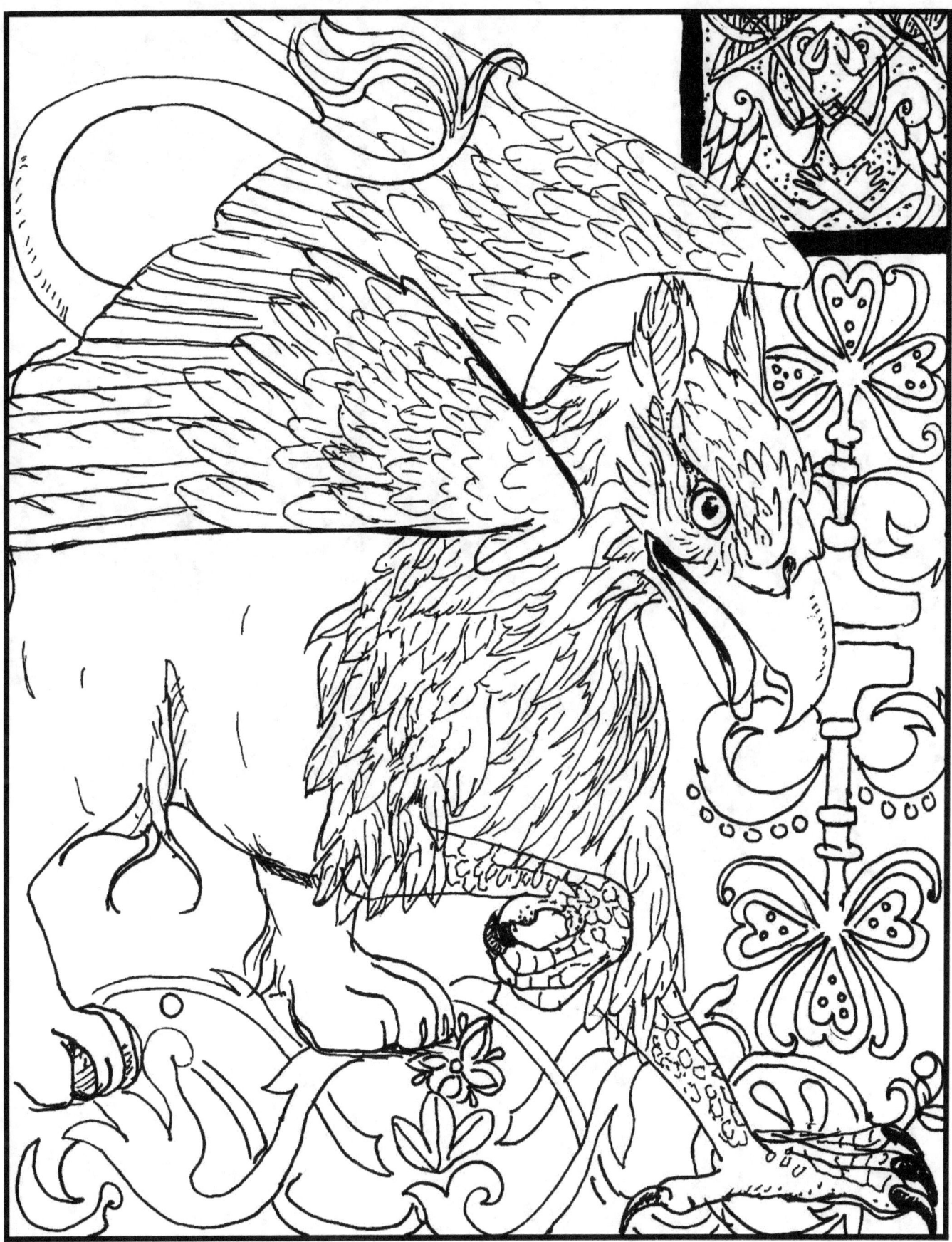

Figure 13 Griffin

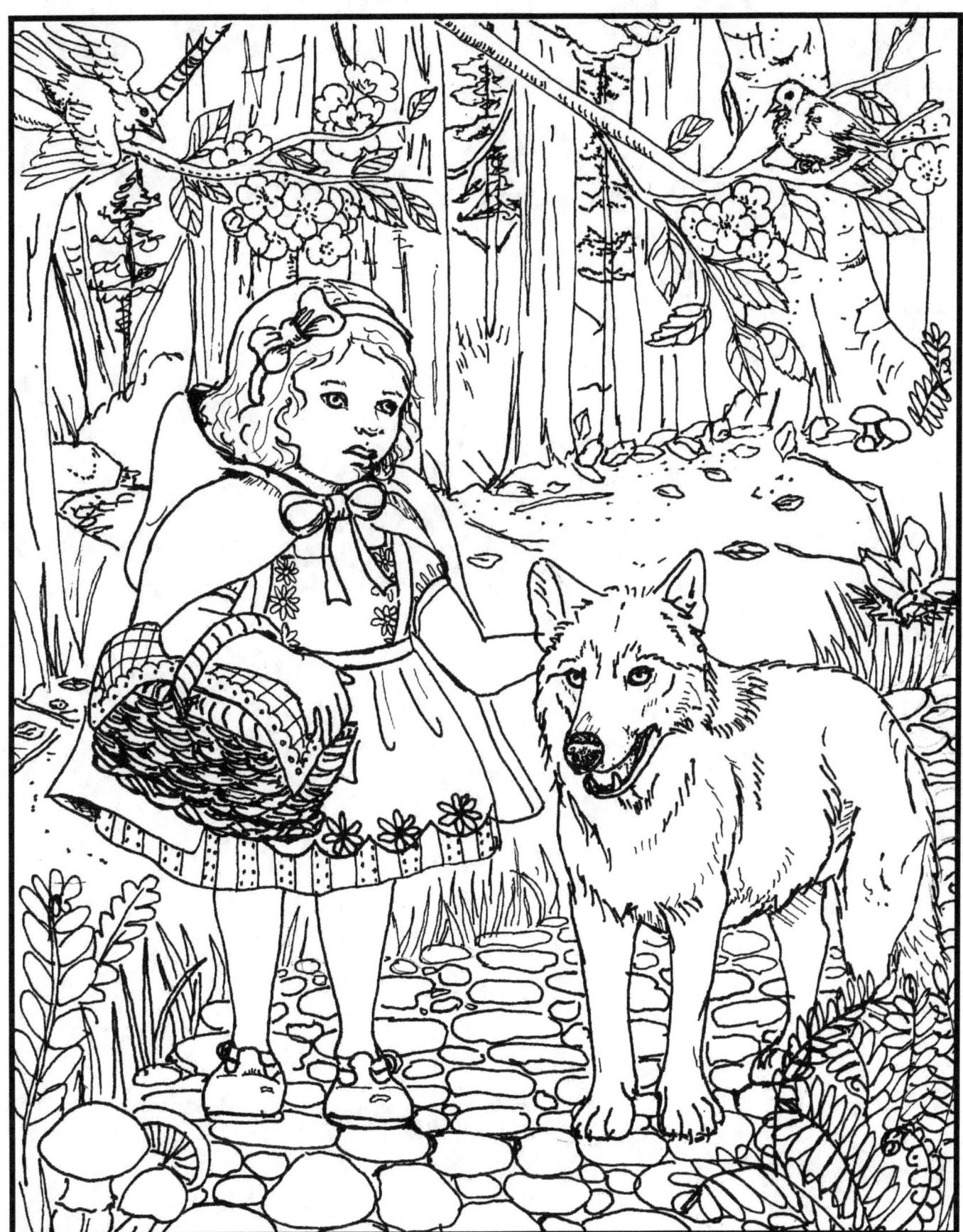

Figure 14 Walk in the Woods

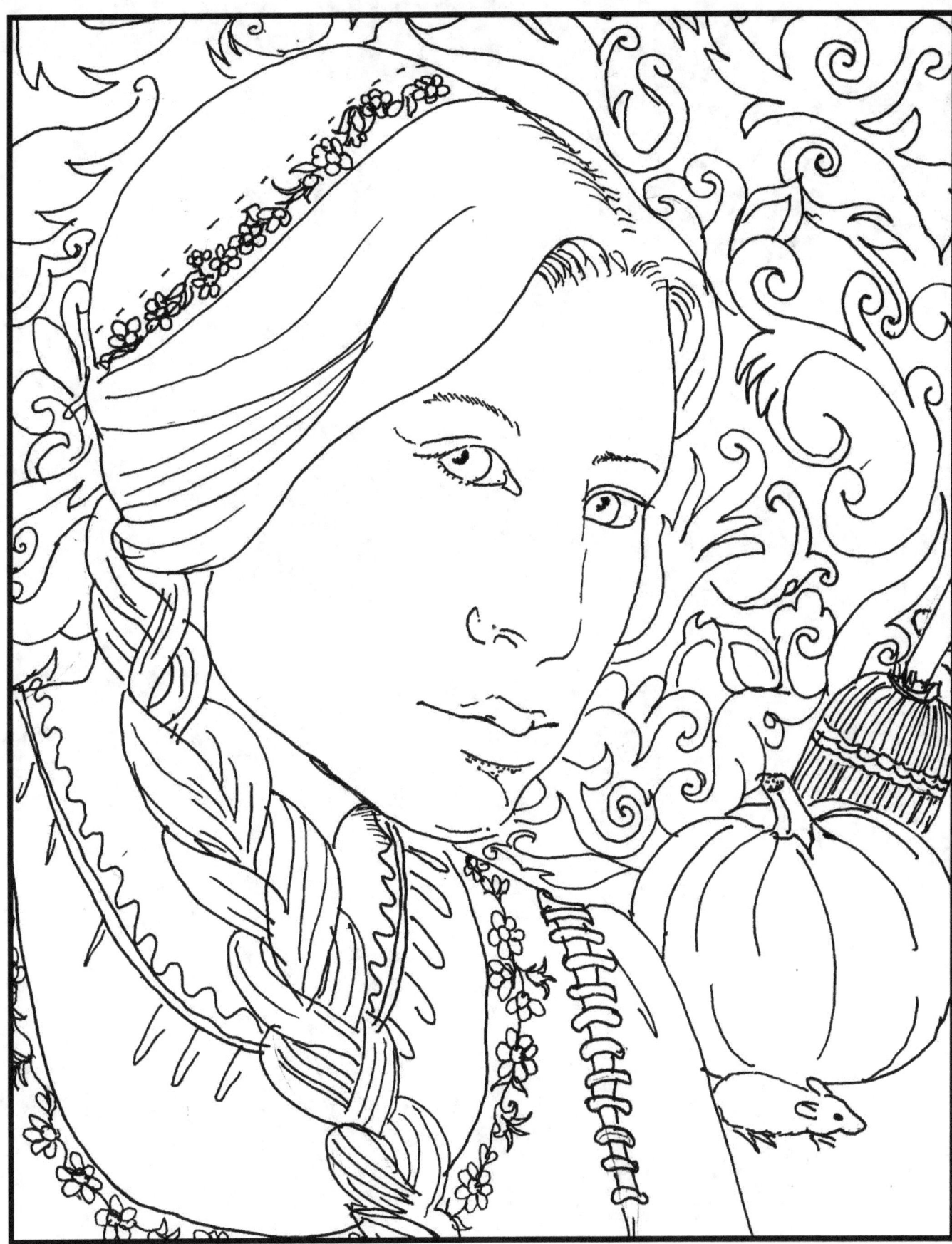

Figure 15 Cinderella

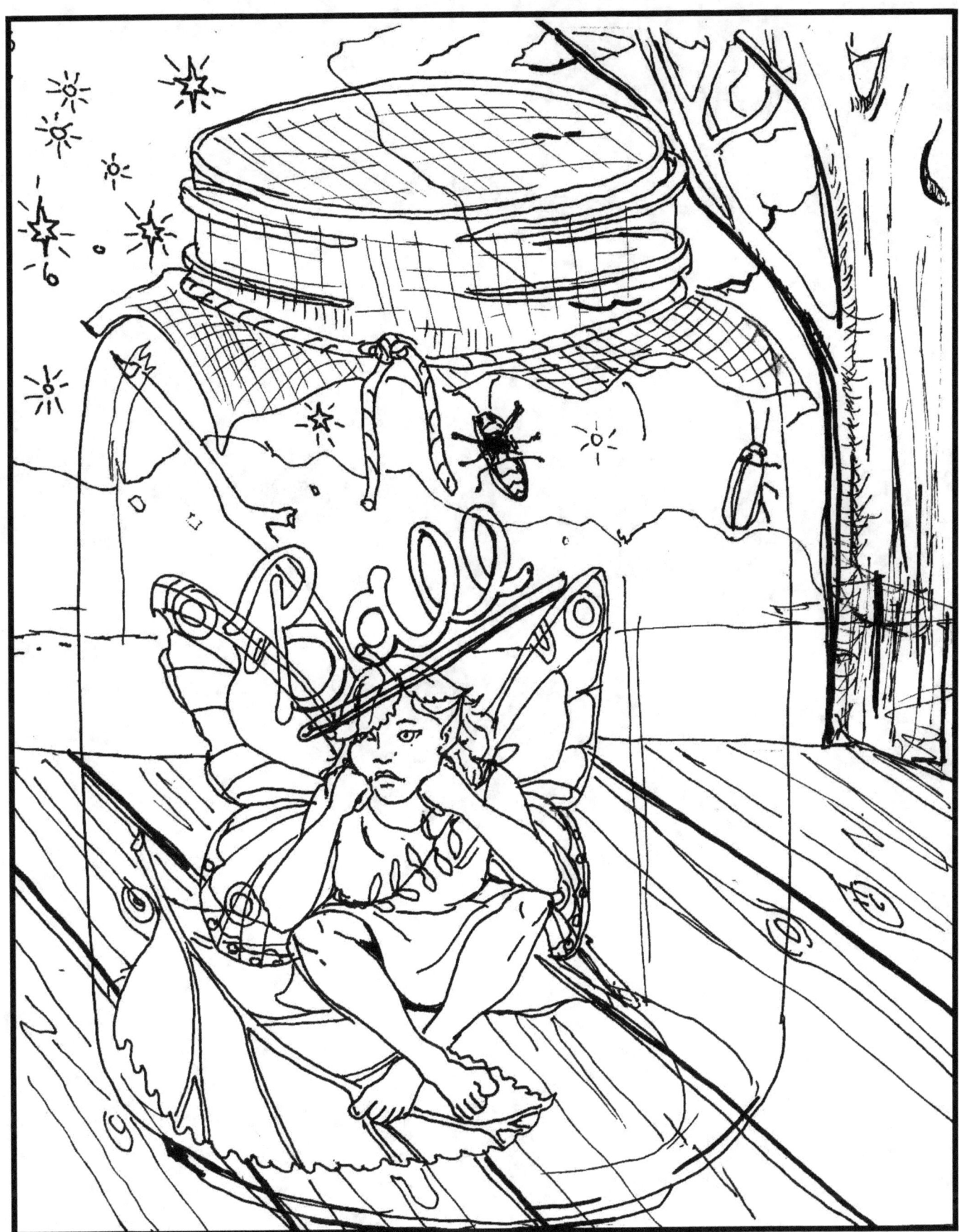

Figure 16 Trapped

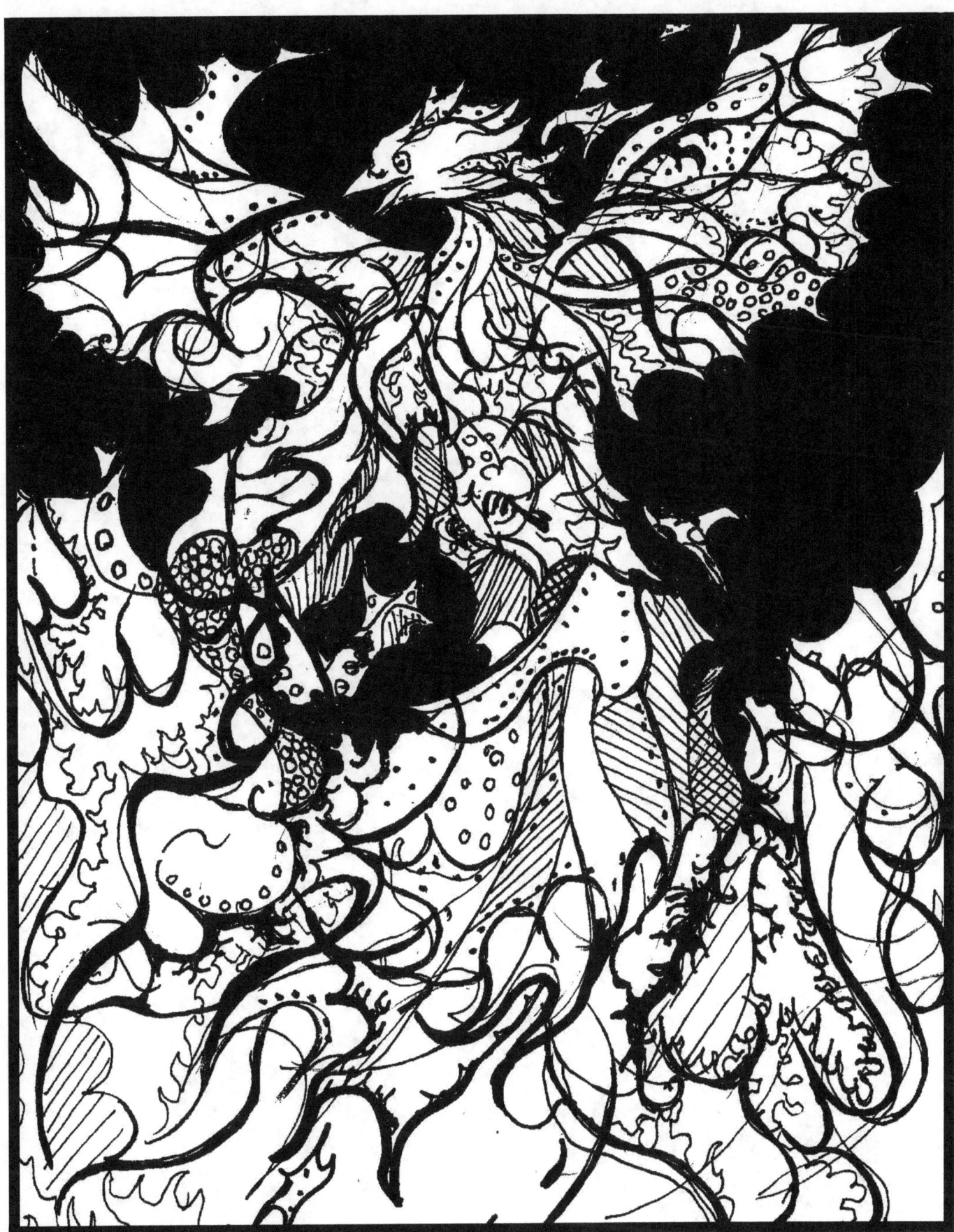

Figure 17 Phoenix

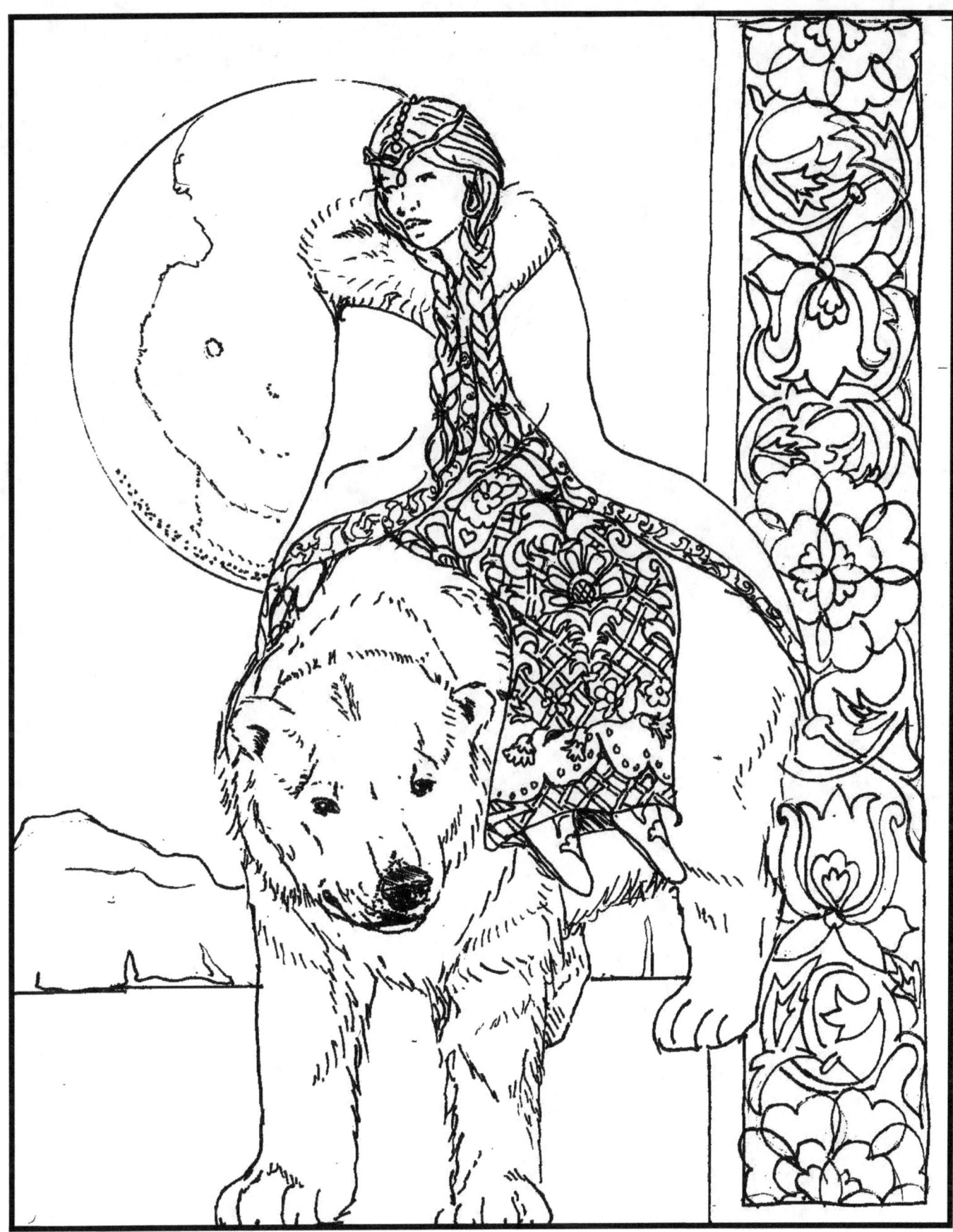

Figure 18 Polar Bear King

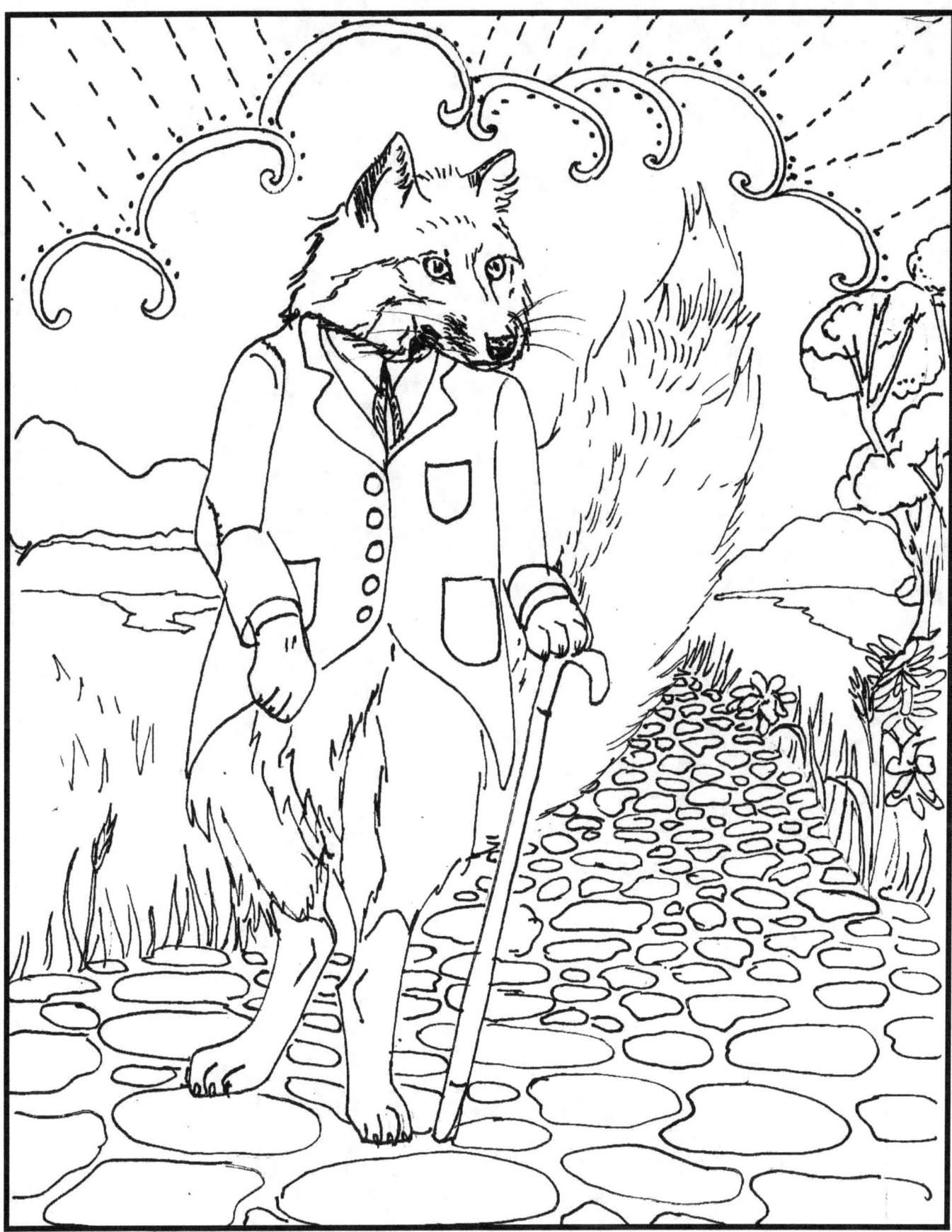

Figure 19 Dapper Fox

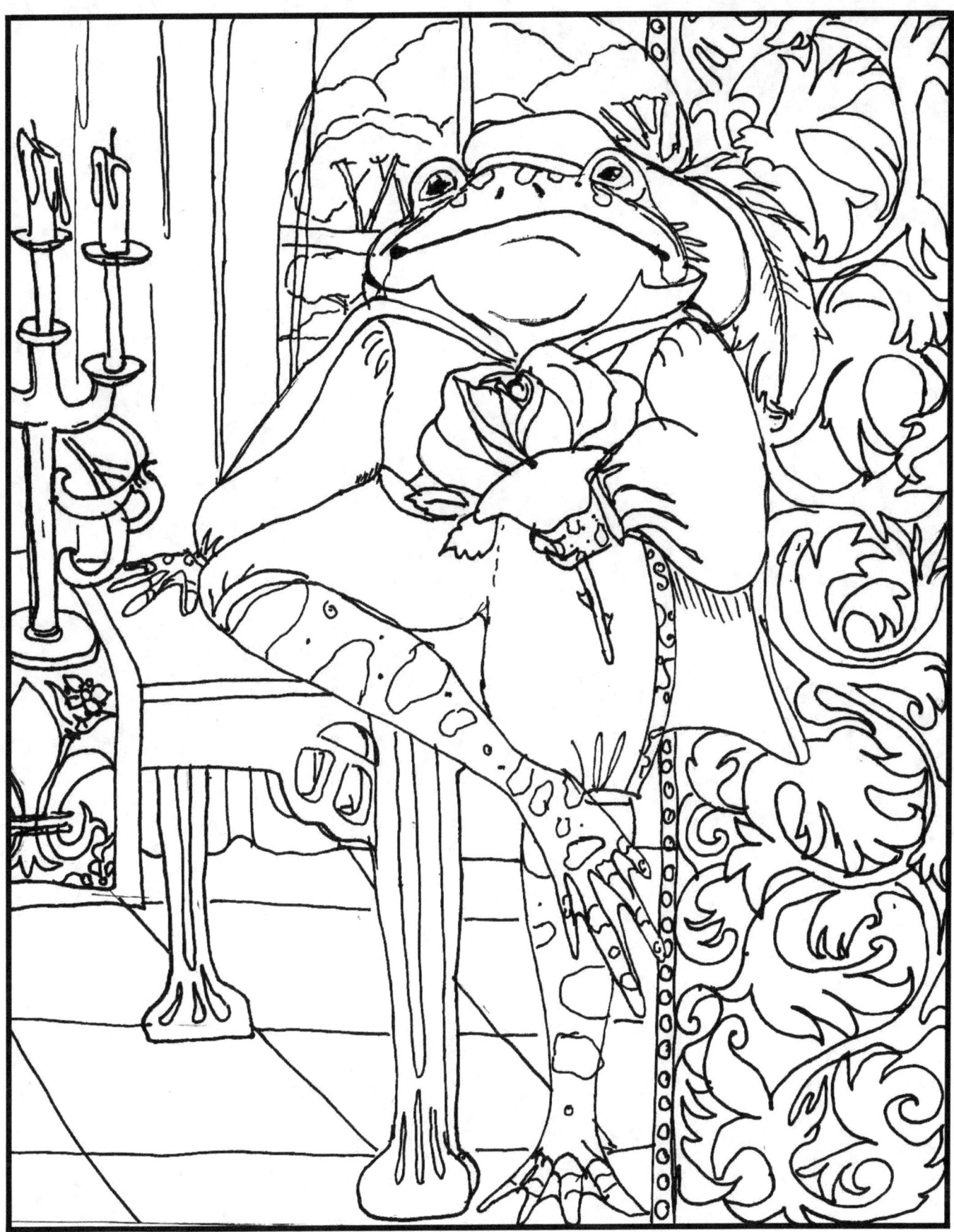

Figure 20 Frog Prince

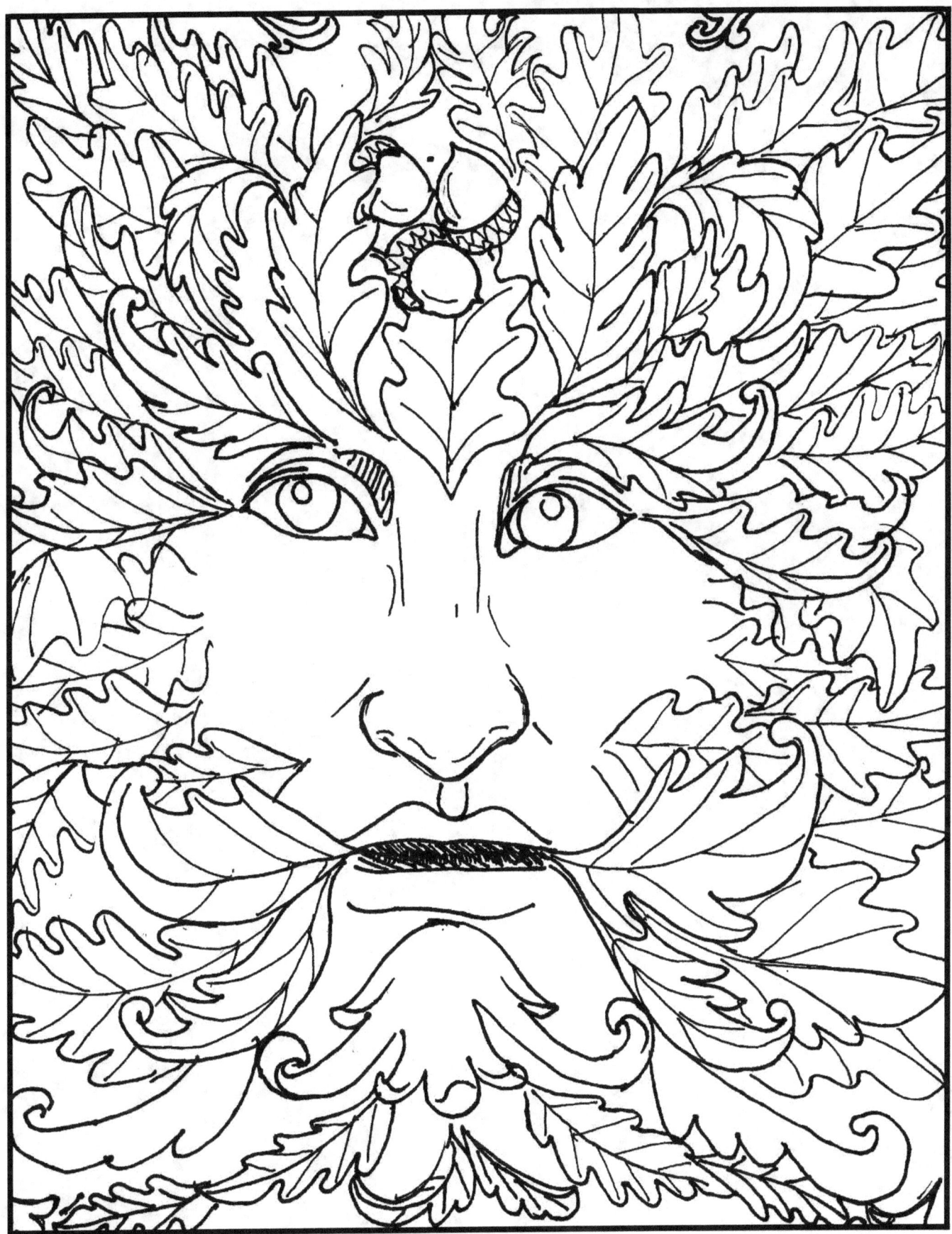

Figure 21 Green Man

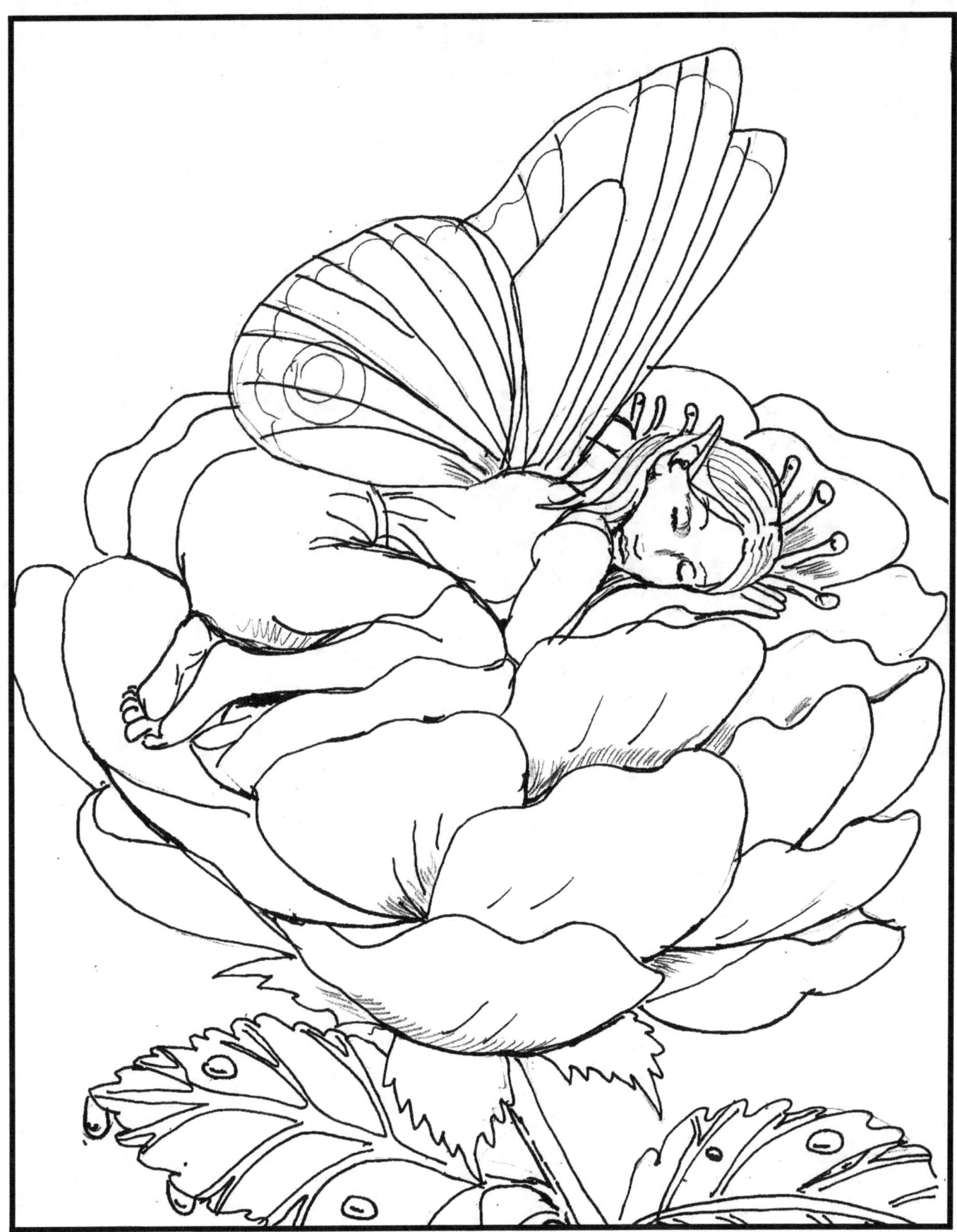

Figure 22 Good Morning

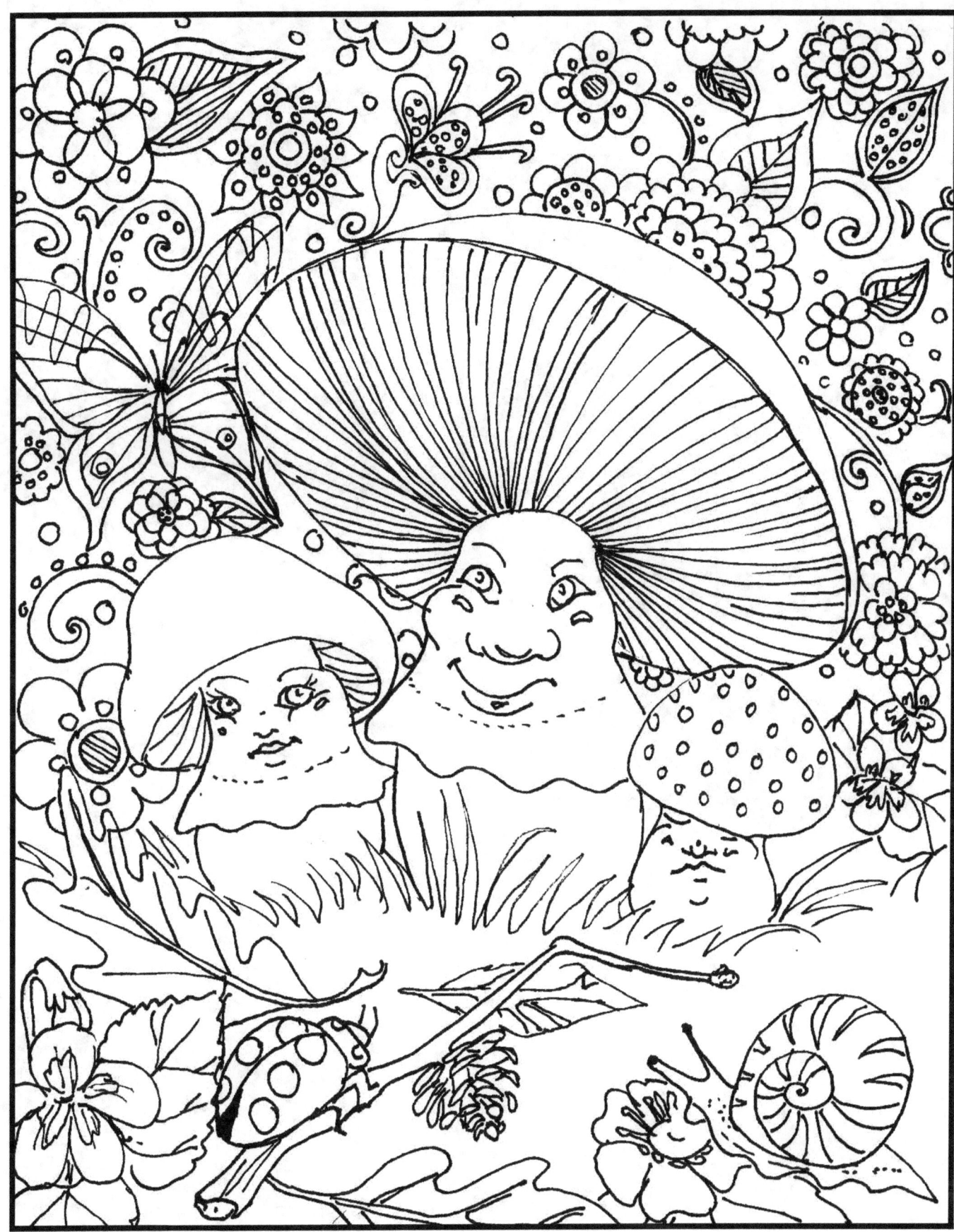

Figure 23 Mushroom People

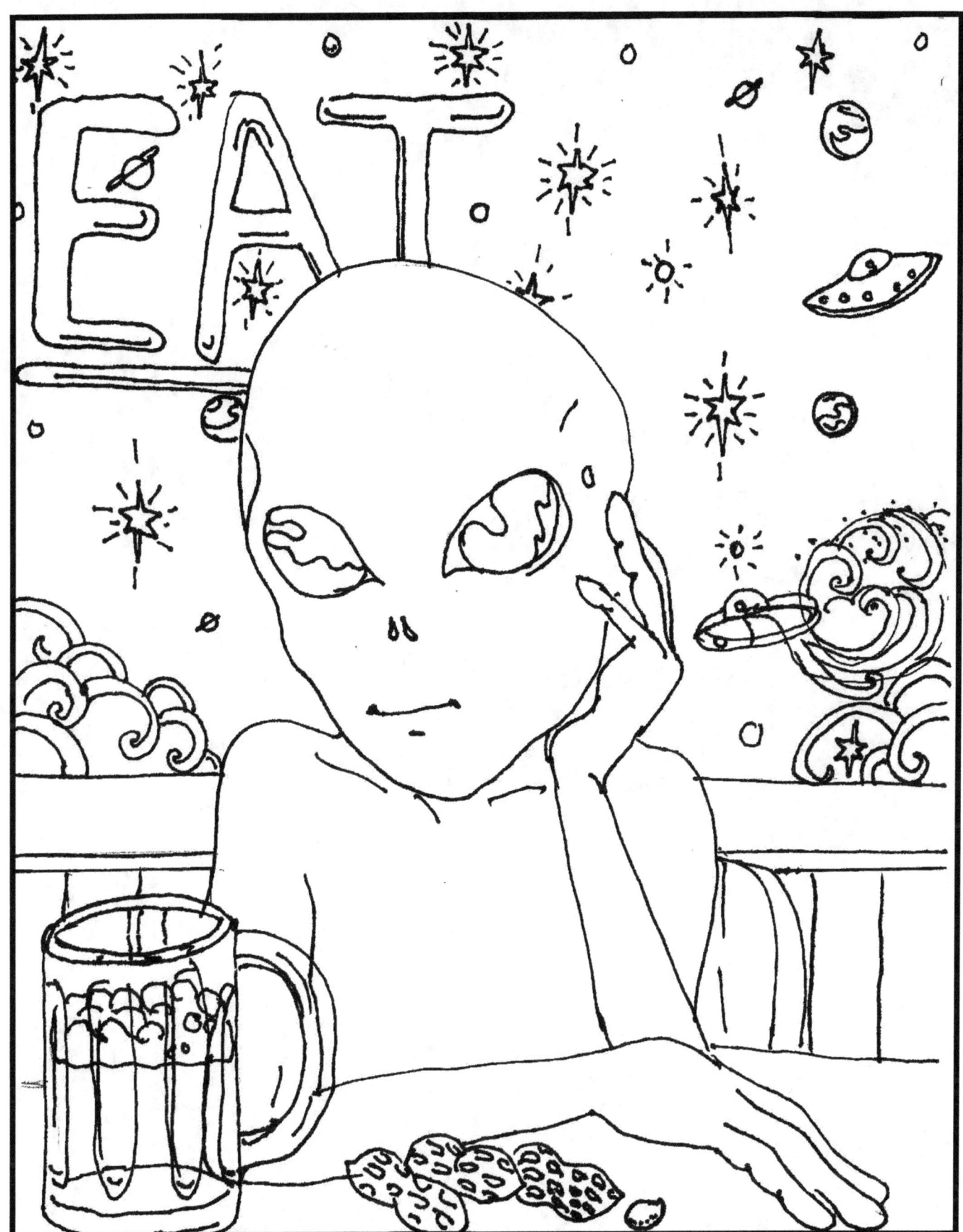

Figure 24 All Night Cafe

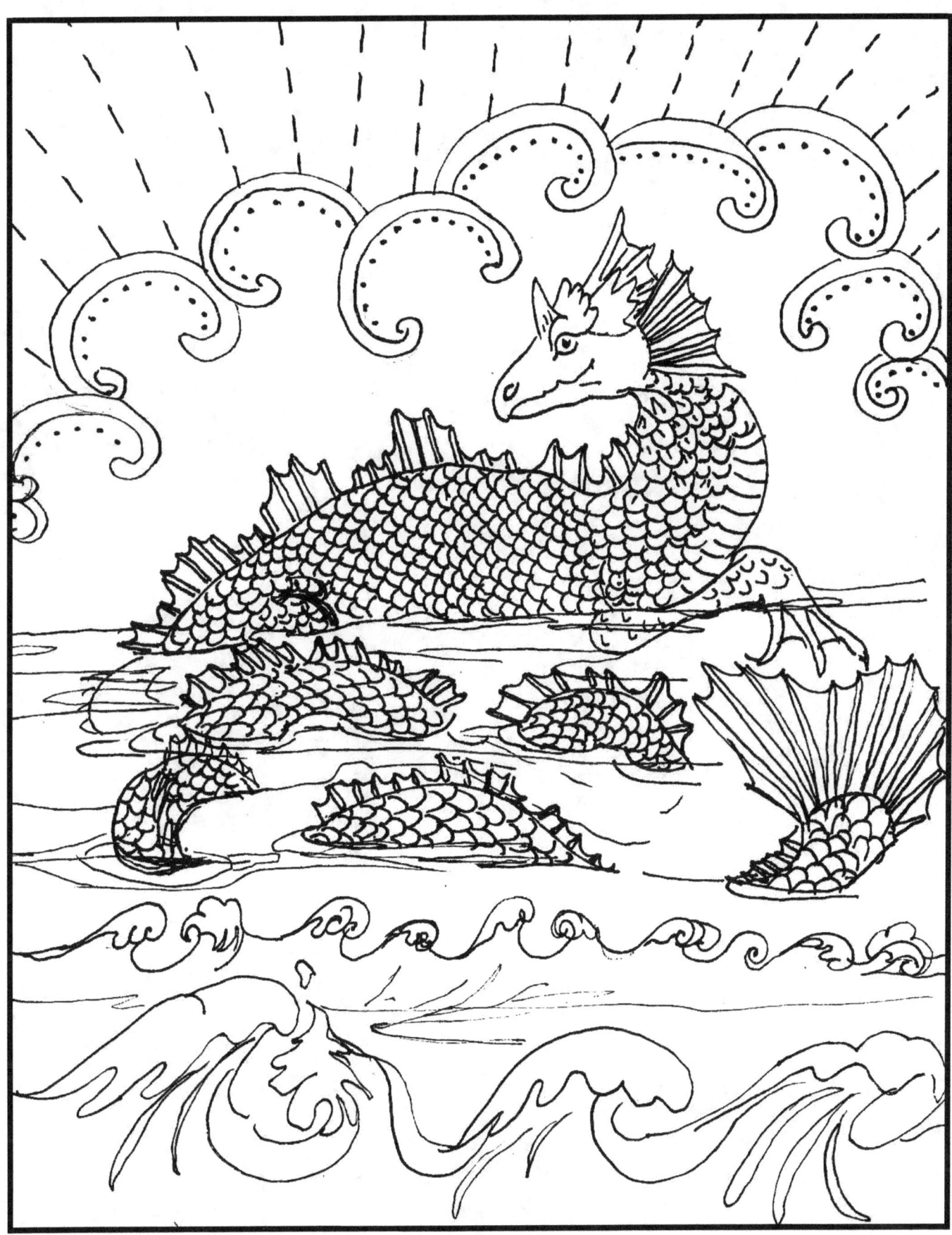

Figure 25 Sea Monster

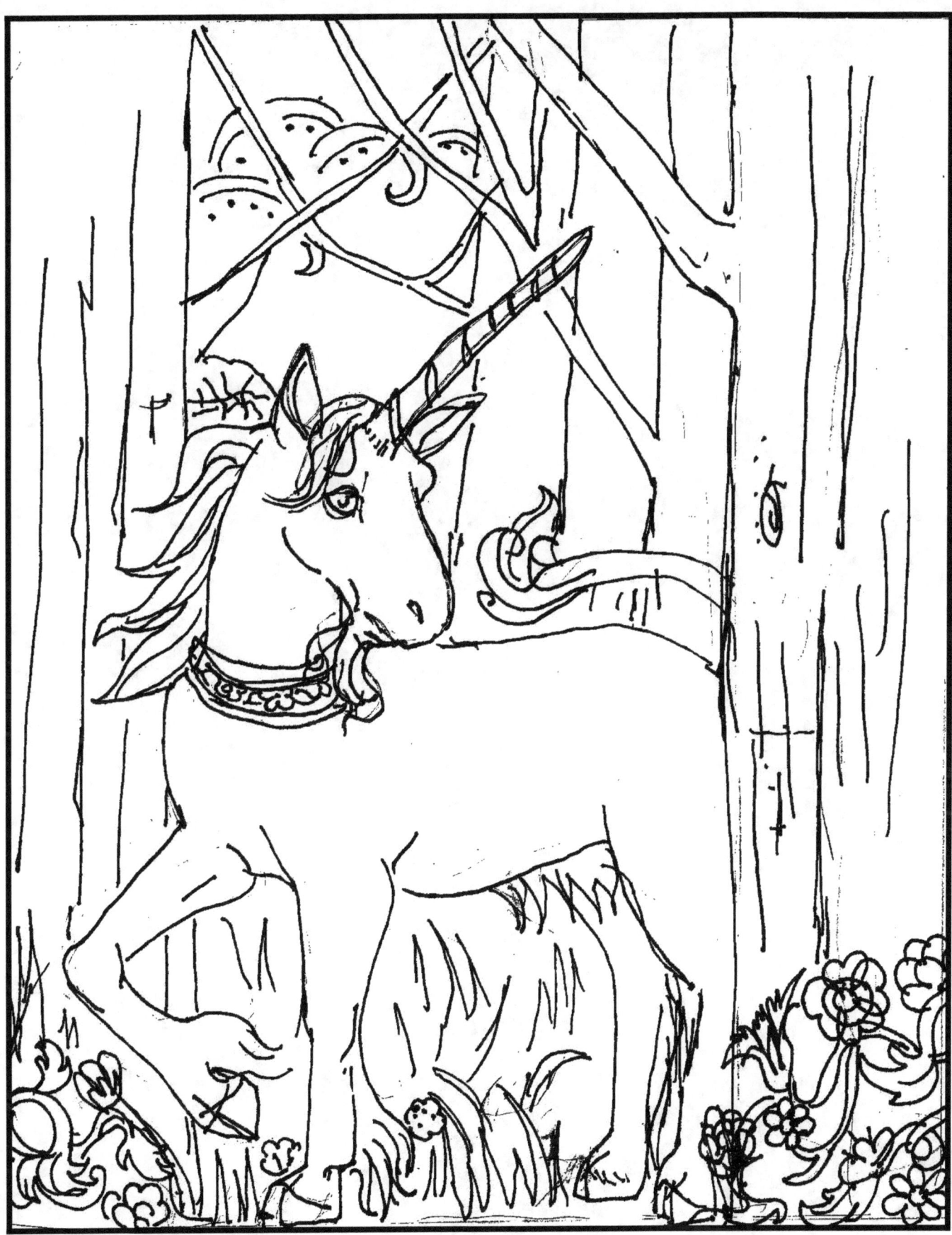

Figure 26 Out of the Woods

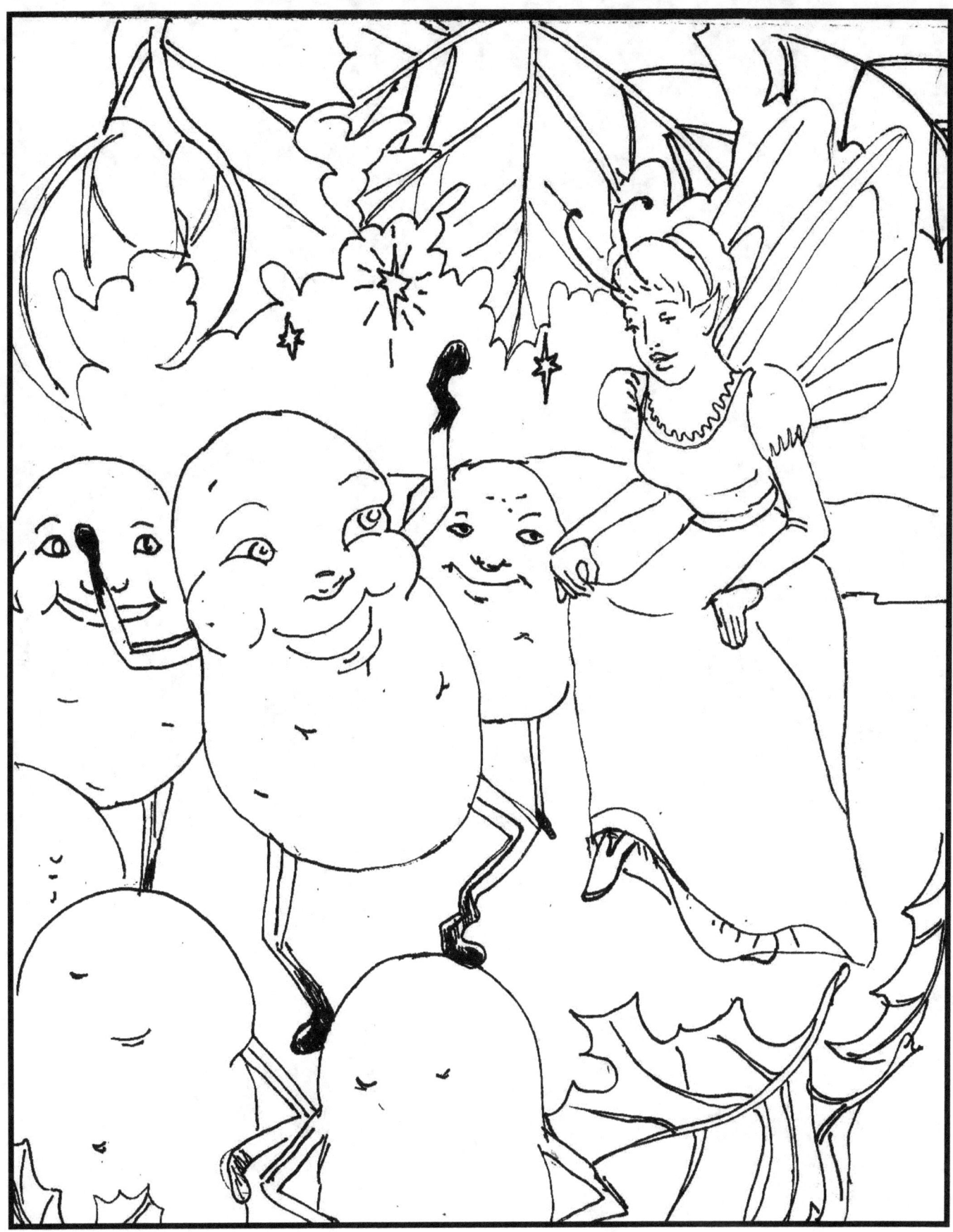

Figure 27 Dance of the Potatoes

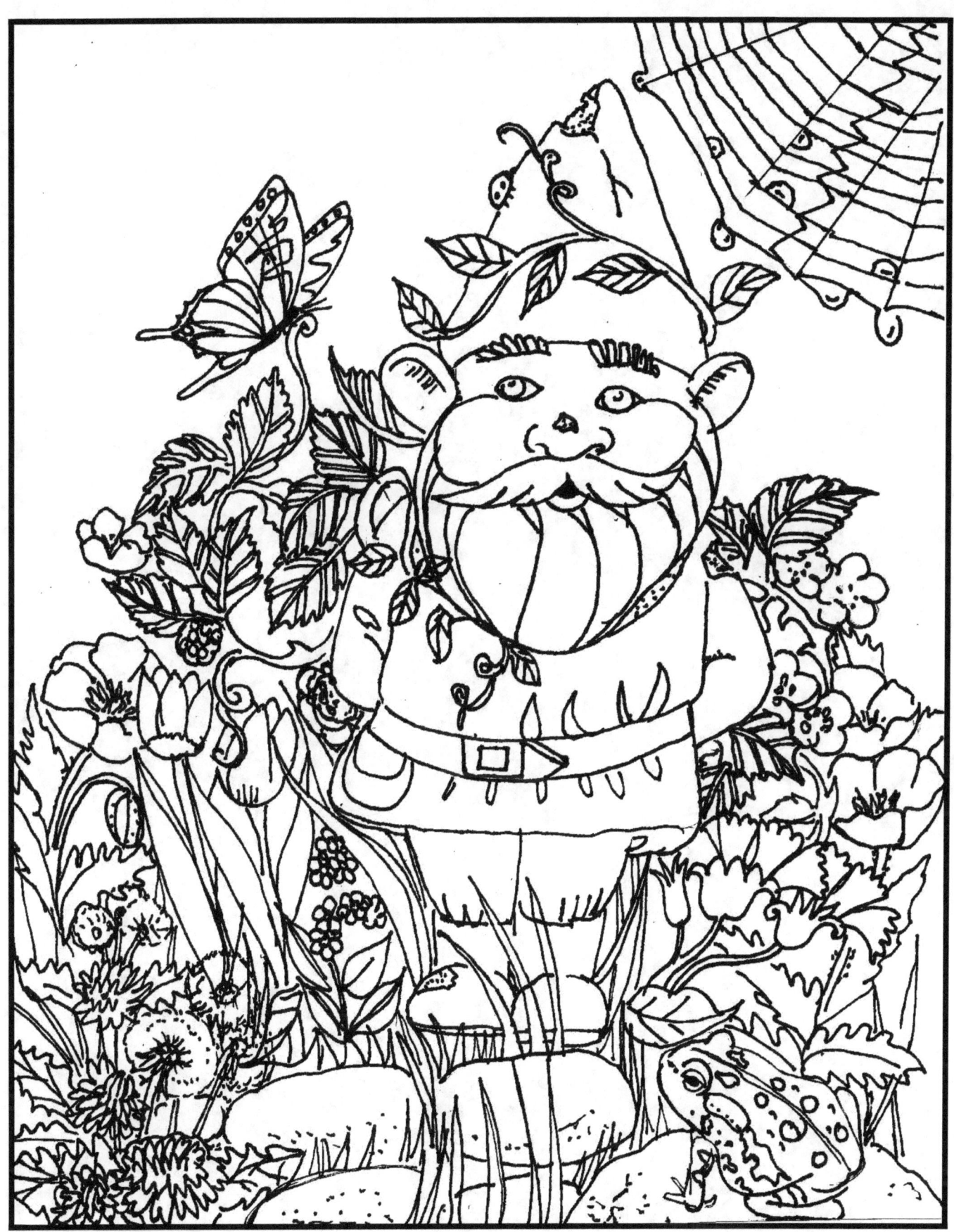

Figure 28 Forgotten Garden Gnome

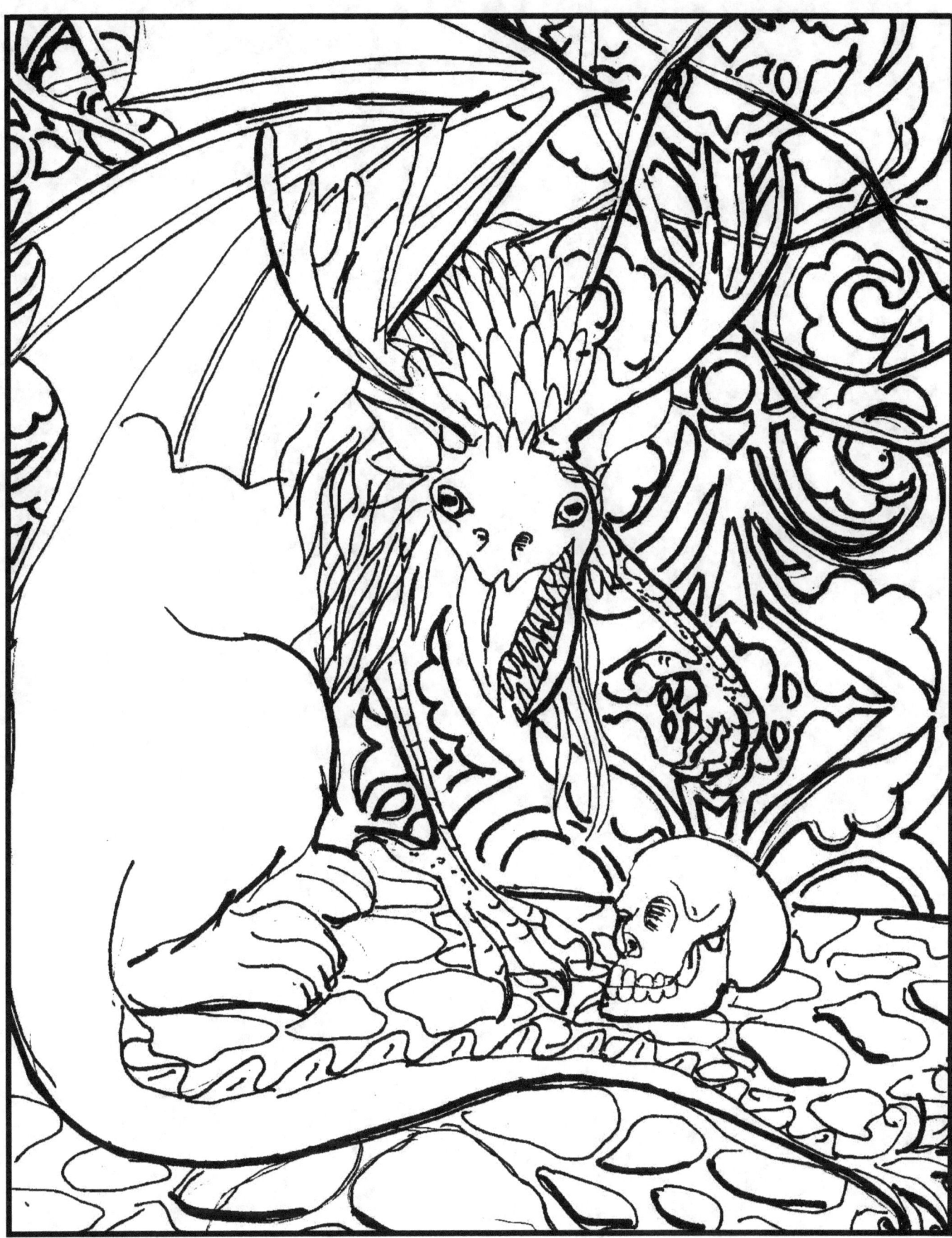

Figure 29 Jabberwocky

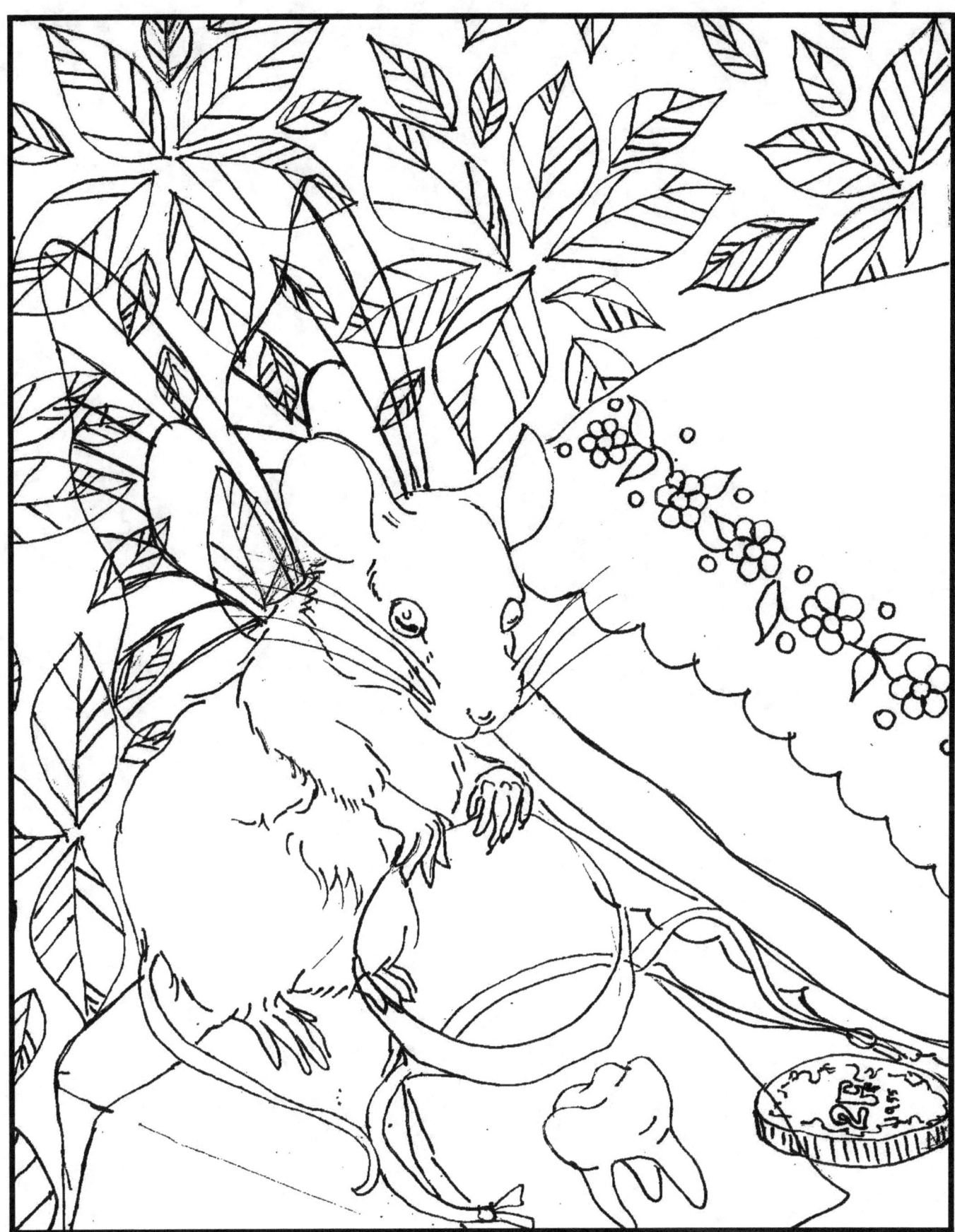

Figure 30 Petite Souris

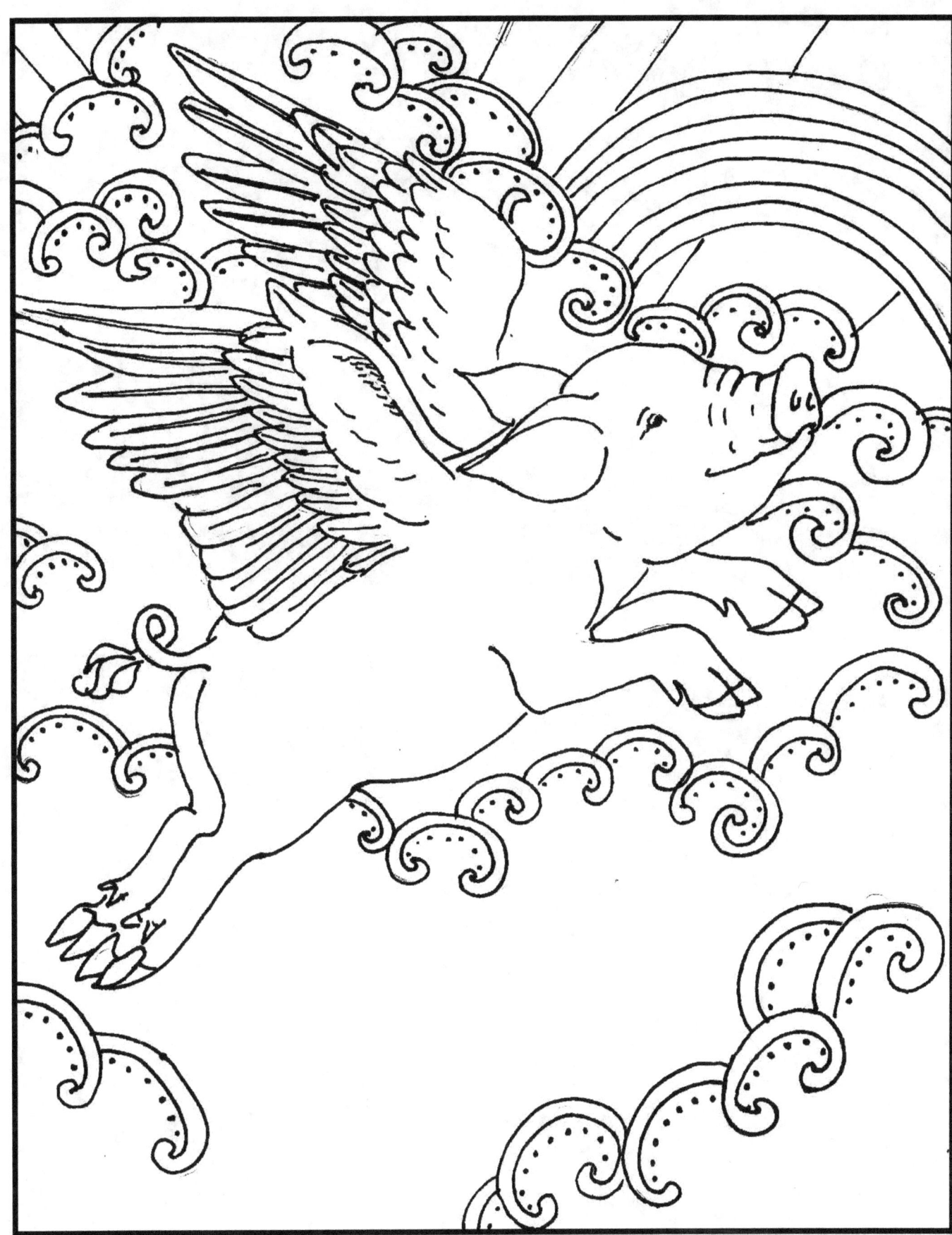

Figure 31 When Pigs Fly

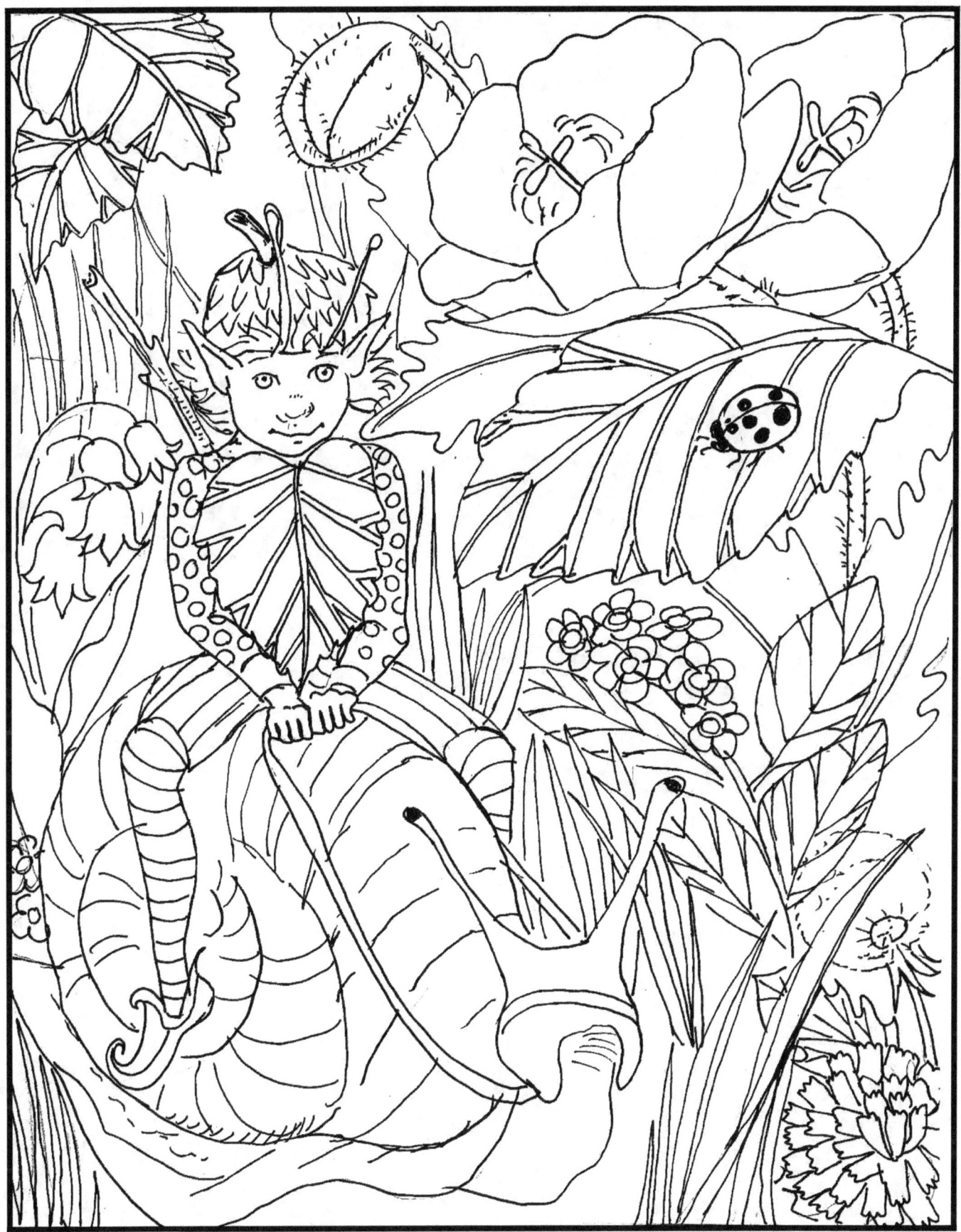

Figure 32 A Ride in the Country

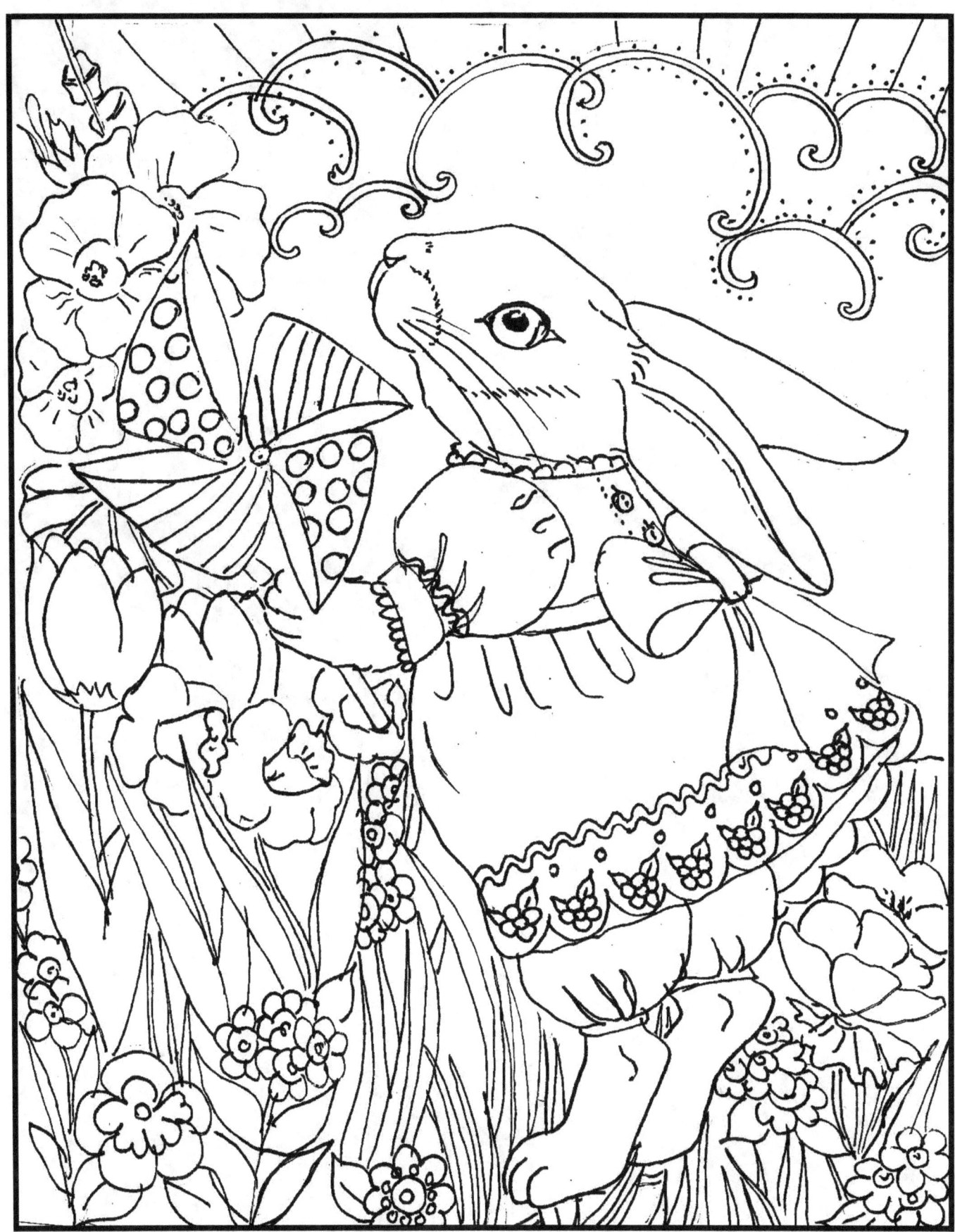

Figure 33 Breezy Spring Morning

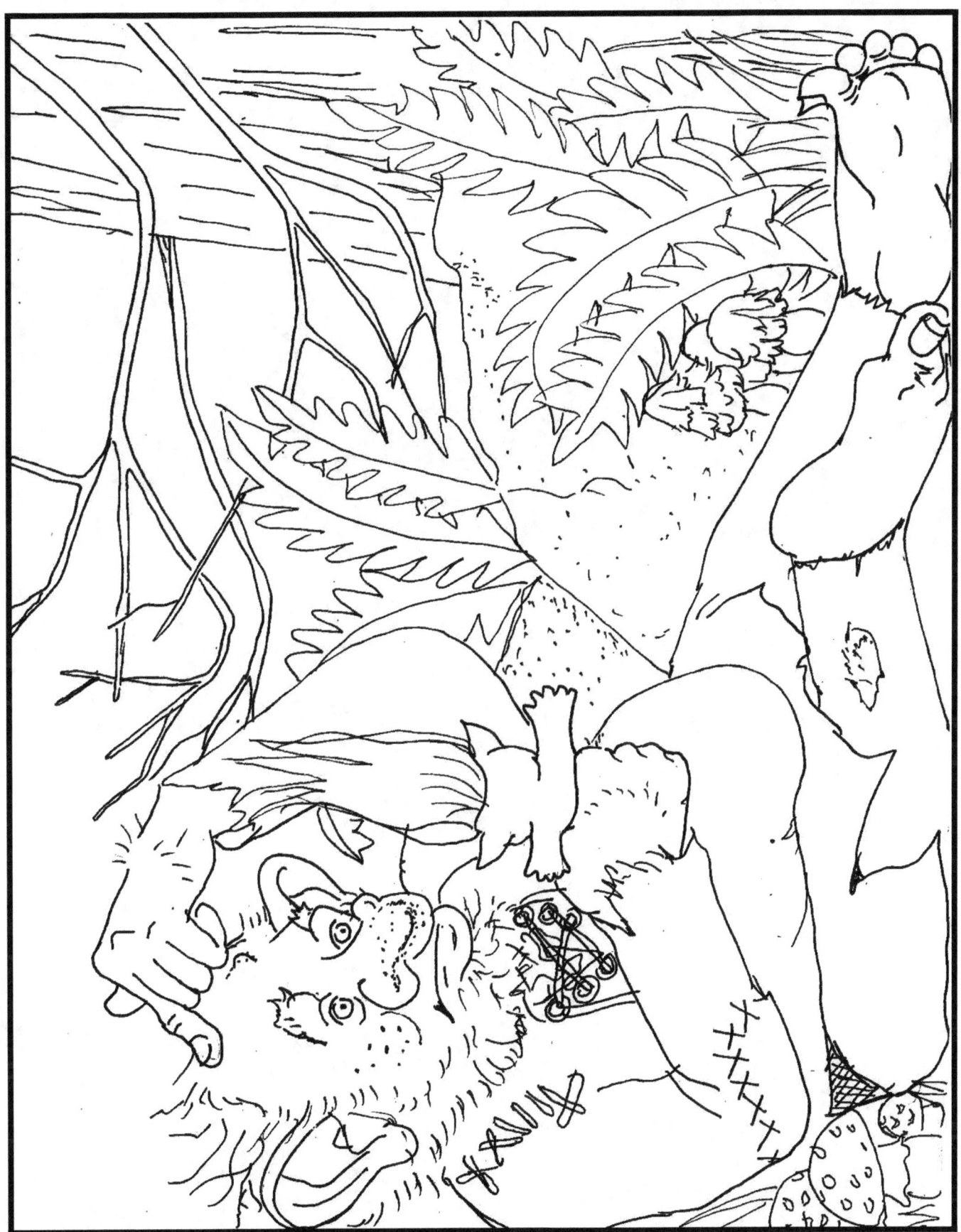

Figure 34 Contemplating Self

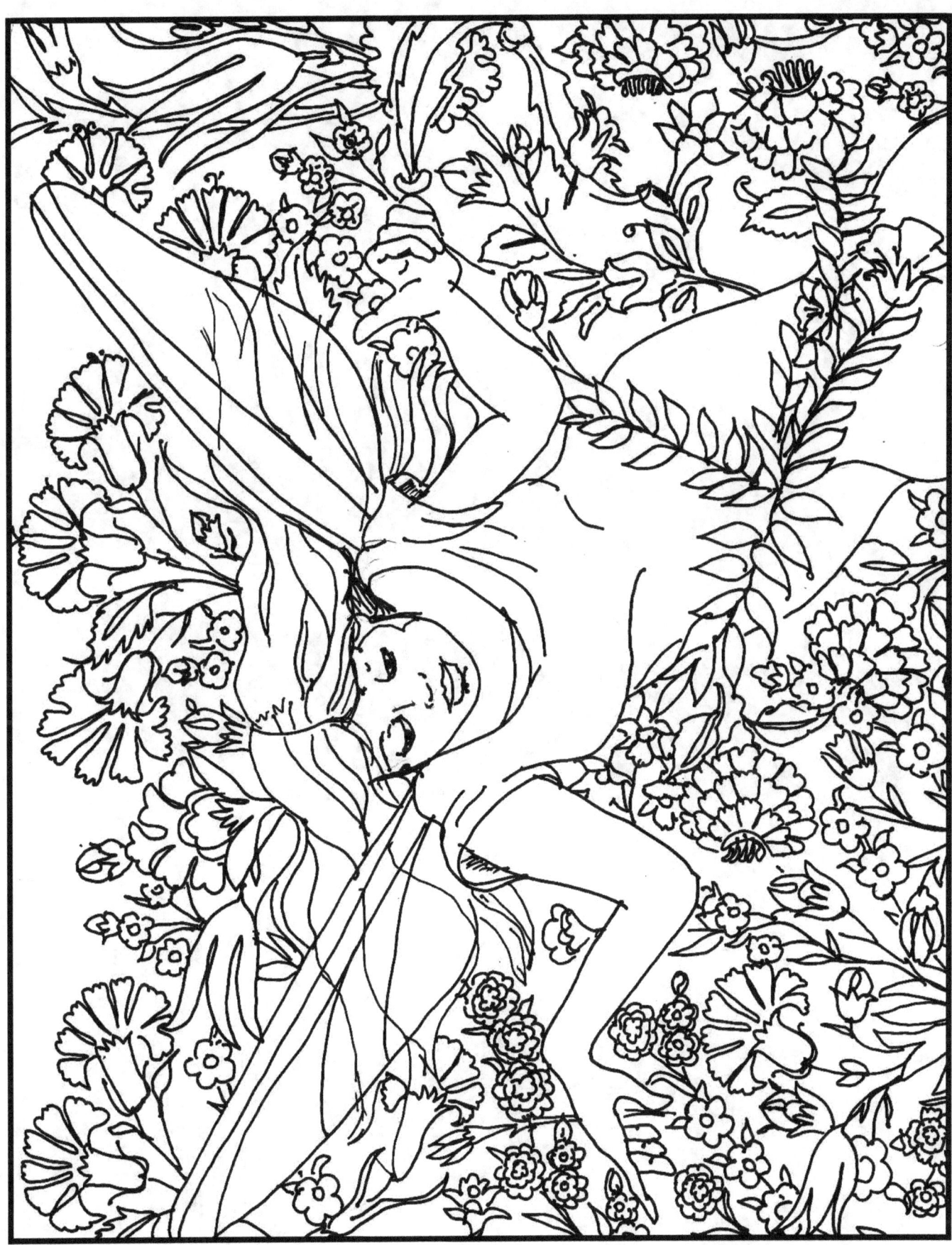

Figure 35 Fairy Flight

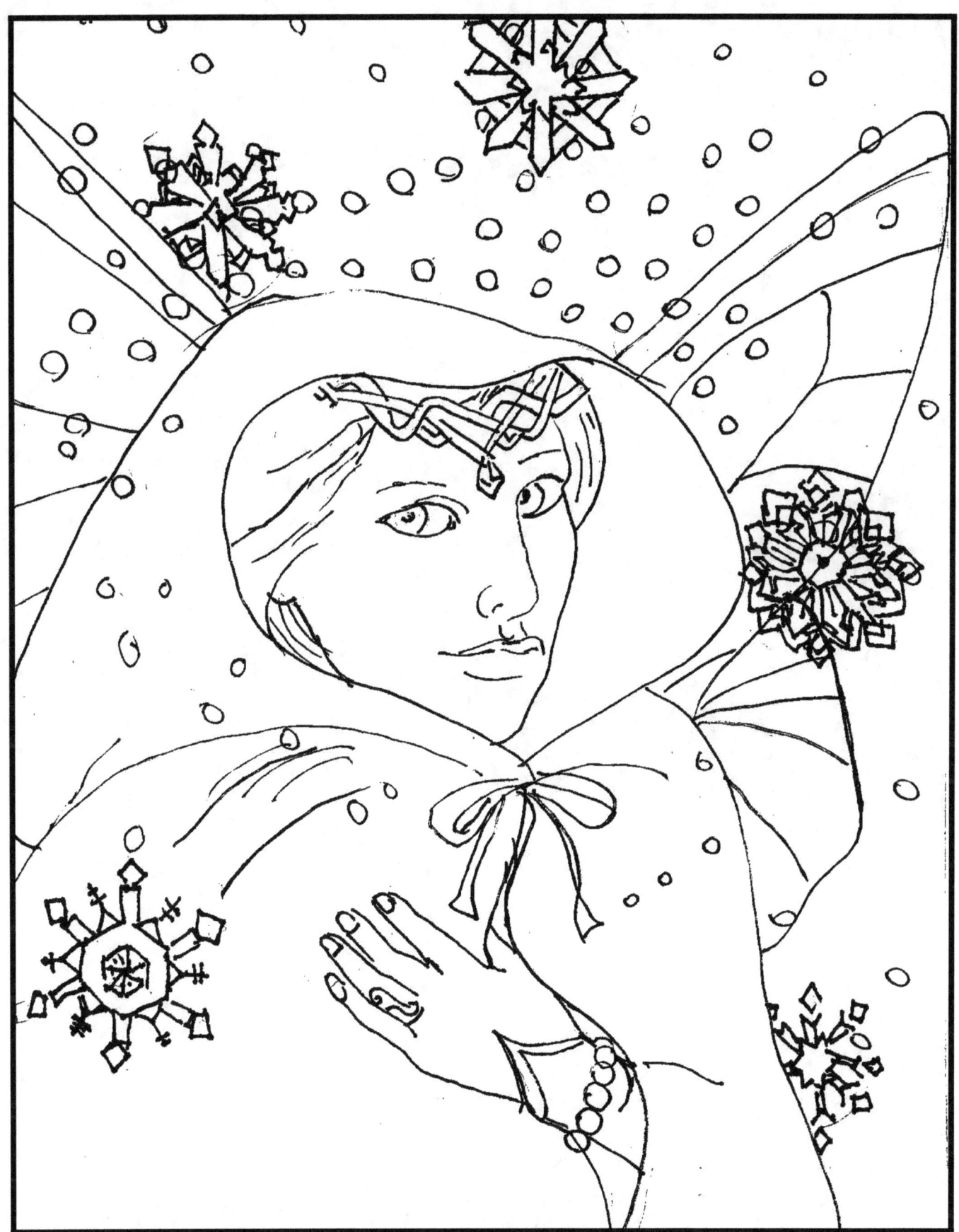

Figure 36 Snowfall

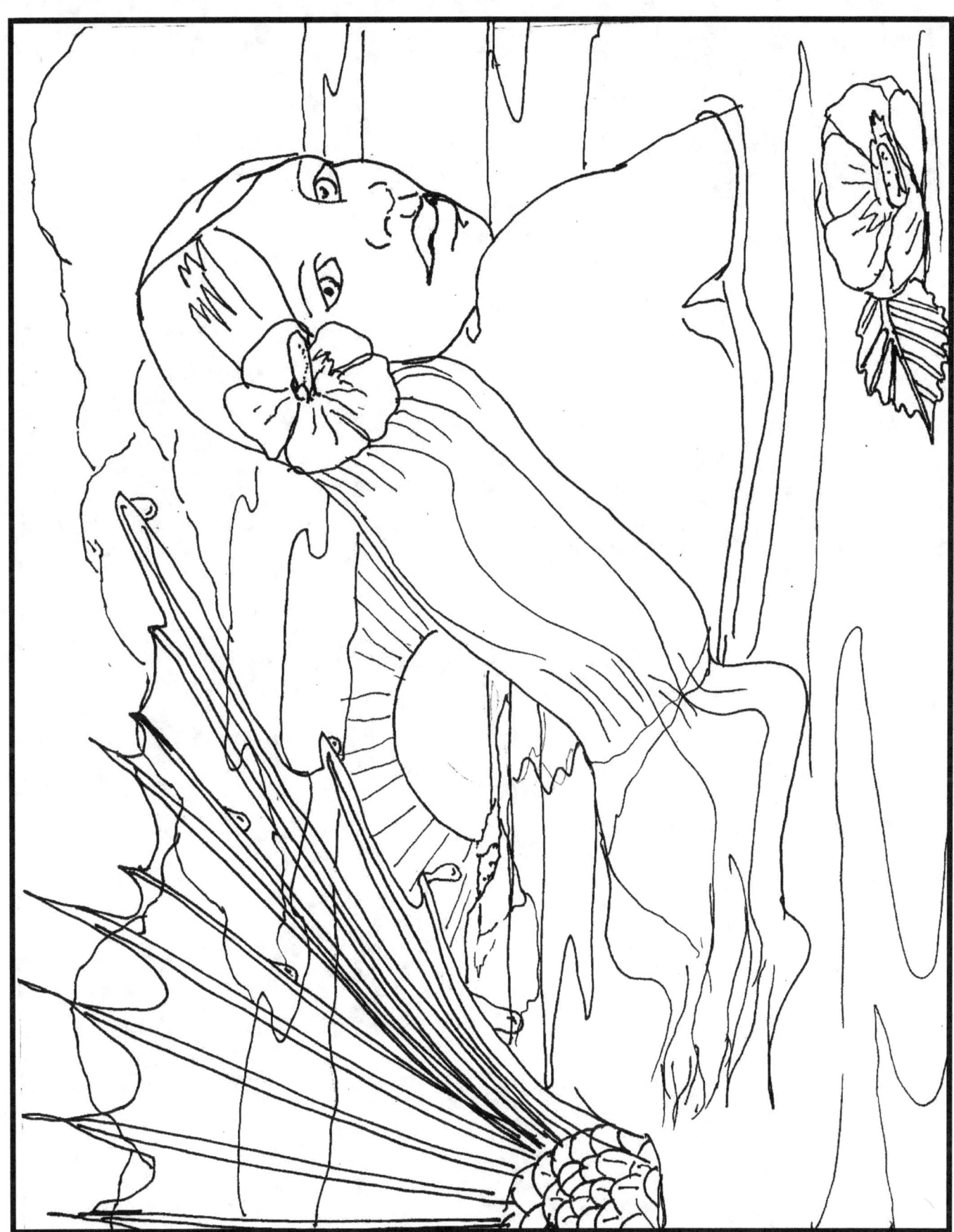

Figure 37 Tropical Paradise

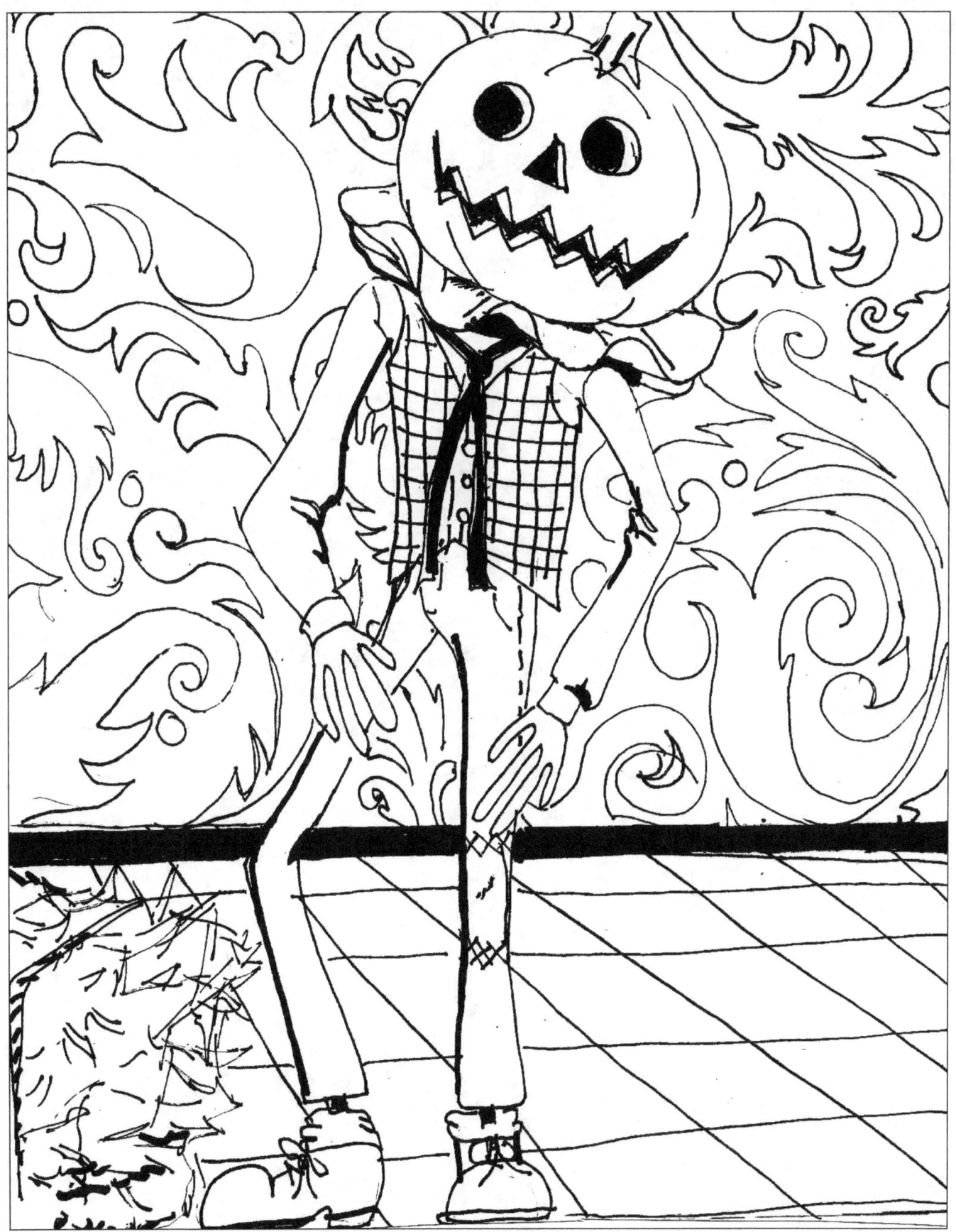

Figure 38 Jack Pumpkin Head

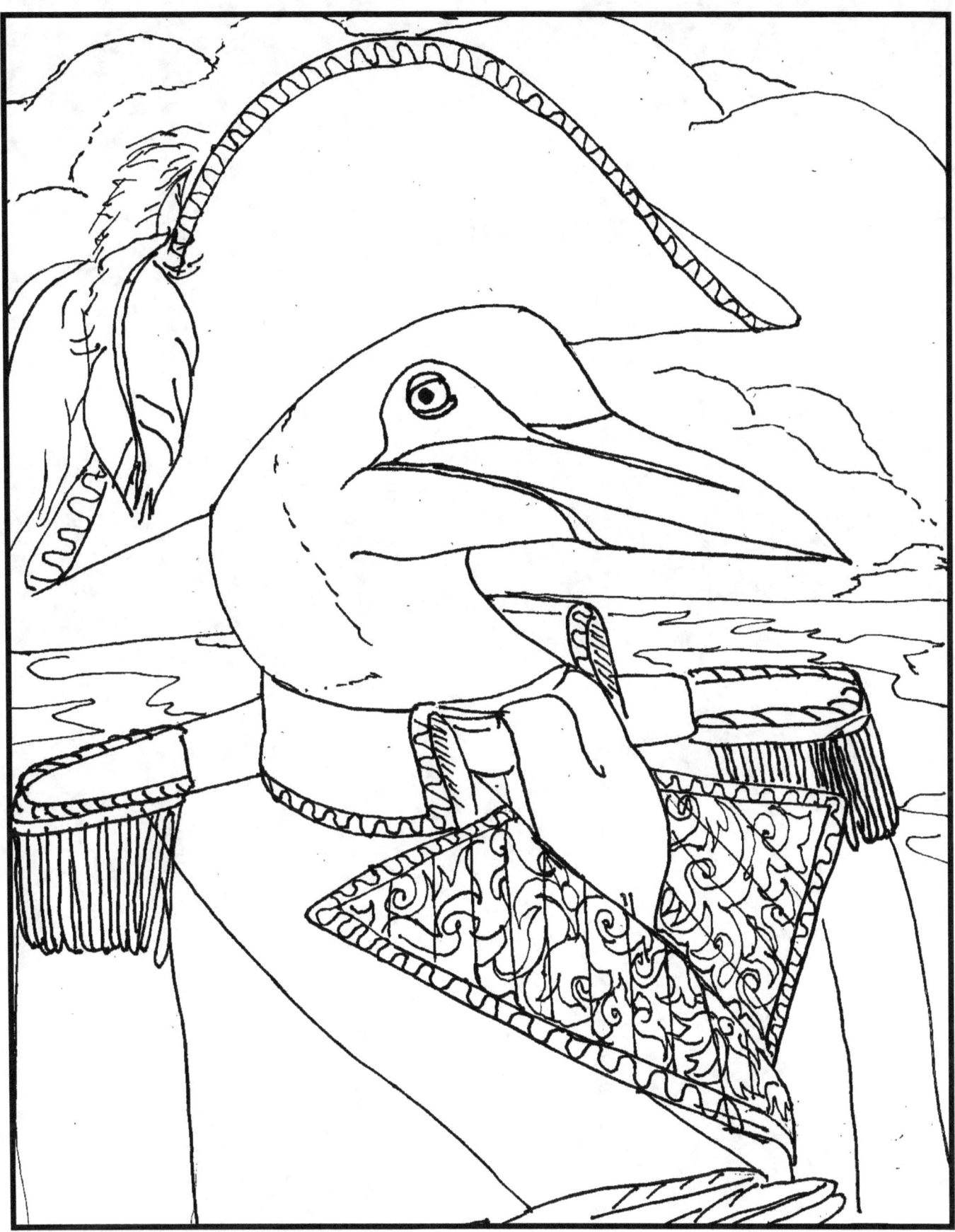

Figure 39 Admiral Bird

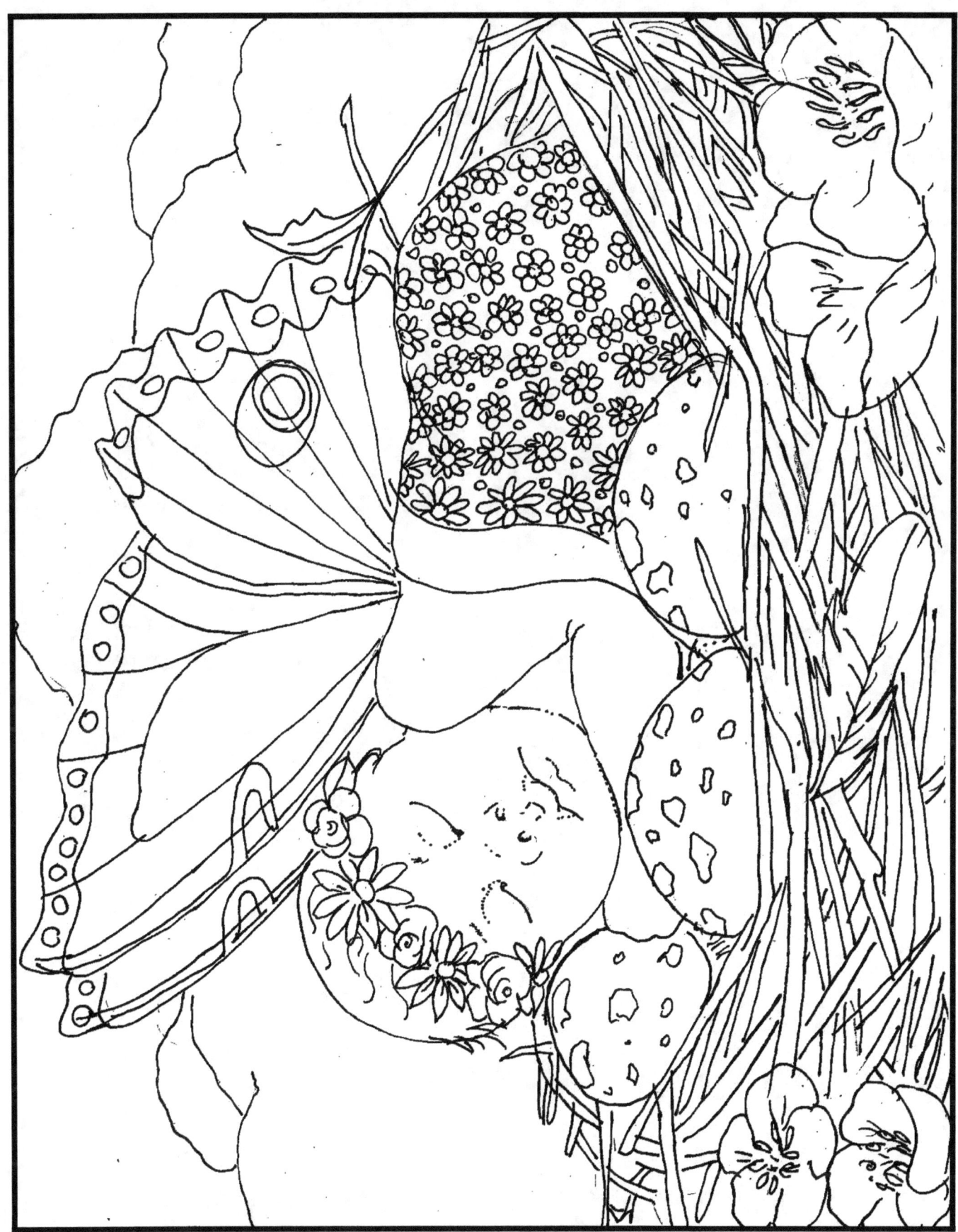

Figure 40 Lullaby

www.ingramcontent.com/pod-product-compliance
Lightning Source LLC
Chambersburg PA
CBHW081608200526
45169CB00021B/2465